the
HELPING
HANDS
HANDBOOK

**A guidebook for kids who want to help
people, animals, and the world we live in**

**Over 100 projects
kids can
really do!**

by patricia adams
and
jean marzollo

illustrated by jeff moores

random house new york

For my parents, Annie Dee and Walton Smith
P. A.

For Cousin Suzie (Mary H. Leger)
J. M.

Text copyright © 1992 by Patricia Adams and Jean Marzollo
Illustrations copyright © 1992 by Jeff Moores

Library of Congress Cataloging-in-Publication Data
Adams, Patricia
The helping hands handbook : a guidebook for kids who want to help people,
animals, and the world we live in / by Patricia Adams and Jean Marzollo ;
illustrated by Jeff Moores.
          p.   cm.
Summary: Describes ways in which children can help at home, in
their community, with the environment, and around the world.
ISBN 0-679-82816-8 (pbk.) — ISBN 0-679-92816-2 (lib. bdg.)
     1. Children as volunteers—United States—Juvenile literature.
      2. Voluntarism—United States—Juvenile literature.
[1. Voluntarism.]   I. Marzollo, Jean.   II. Moores, Jeff, ill.   III. Title.
            HQ784.V64A33   1992
            302'.14—dc20   91-42947

Manufactured in the United States of America
10 9 8 7 6 5 4 3 2 1

Contents

Introduction:
Kid Power

life can be a wonderful experience, full of joy, love, and satisfaction. And one of the best experiences of all is the experience of giving.

Imagine yourself reaching out and helping to solve the world's problems. Poverty, ignorance, illiteracy, loneliness, illness, pollution—what if *you* could help to end them? Wouldn't that be great? But what can you really do? After all, you're only a kid!

Many kids just like you ask these questions every day. The world is full of kids who want more than anything to help—to lend a helping hand. You'll be in good company when you reach out with them.

When you lend a hand, you start to feel powerful. Whether you work individually, in small groups, or in conjunction with large organizations, you can make an impact on the causes you choose. Your contribution has power because you are not alone. Other kids like you throughout the world are making contri-

butions, and there's no doubt about it:
kid power works. Lots of kids helping in
the world can do a lot!

Whom should you help?
You've made up your mind to help—to
really do something. But whom or what
should you help? Give yourself time to
answer that question. Survey the possi-
bilities. You may want to focus upon the
one area in which you are most interested: your community, needy people,
animals, Mother Earth, foreign countries,
or national politics. Or you may want to
help different causes at different times.
However you choose to proceed, you'll
find that this book will guide you. *The
Helping Hands Handbook* will tell you
what other kids like you have done and
will provide you with the information
you need to get started.

> *To look up and not down,*
> *To look forward and not back,*
> *To look out and not in, and*
> *To lend a hand.*
> —Edward Everett Hale

As you're considering different areas
in which you might lend a hand, listen

to the world. Where are the calls for help coming from in *your* community? In your state? In your country? Which voices tug the most at your heart? Some kids feel drawn to end the suffering of animals. Some feel drawn to help the ill in hospitals or the starving children in distant lands. No one cause is better than another. Find the one that you think you can help best and will give you the most satisfaction.

If you want to change the world, start small.
—Peace Corps advertisement

One way to ensure the success of your project is to start small. There's no way you can solve all the problems of the world. Pick an activity that you're sure you can deal with and a time frame that is reasonable. If your plan seems overwhelming, simplify it. When you become more experienced at helping the world, you can take on more complex projects.

Be aware, as you plan, that things may go wrong. A blizzard may fall on the day of your bake sale. The beach you cleaned up one week may become littered the next. Sometimes you just have to be patient. If you work with others, you'll be able to share the frustrations as well as the fun, and that will make you feel better. No one ever said it would be easy! Just rewarding.

There is a destiny which makes us brothers,
None goes his way alone;
All that we send into the lives of others
Comes back into our own.
—Source unknown

5

How you can help

There are four main ways to help the world: through service, through financial donations, through your purchasing power, and through influence.

*We have much more to offer
than we may realize. All we have to do is ask,
"How can I help?" with an open heart,
and then really listen.*
—Ram Dass and Paul Gorman

● **provide service**
You can help the world by volunteering to do a job that needs to get done, such as planting community gardens, helping someone learn to read, or shelving books at the library. In this book you'll find many ideas for serving your community, animals, the Earth, and people in other countries.

● **give financial donations**
You can help the world by donating money to organizations that help the world. Many well-known agencies use only adult volunteers. They do not have

specific work that kids can help them do, but they welcome donations from kids enthusiastically. You'll find fund-raising ideas throughout *The Helping Hands Handbook*, but if fund-raising is your primary interest, you will find help in Chapter Nine: "When Money Talks Loudest: Fund-Raising Ideas."

● *use your purchasing power*
You may not think your weekly allowance or the money you have to buy things is powerful, but it is! According to *The New York Times*, kids have an impact on the United States economy that totals about $230 billion per year. You can be an educated consumer. When you shop, you have the power to affect our environment. You can refuse to buy foods wrapped in polystyrene or non-biodegradable plastic, heavily packaged products, and products that depend on harsh experiments using animals. "Think green!" so that you don't support products that cause harm to Earth or the people and animals who share the planet with you. Ryan Eliason of Santa Cruz, California, is a member of YES (Youth for Environmental Sanity), an environmental organization that includes more than

100,000 junior high and high school students. He says, "It feels powerful. If you're saying to a company, 'No, I don't like what you're doing and I'm not going to support it,' you feel strong."

● *influence others*
You influence others by the way you live your life. If you throw away your food wrappers in a trash can, your friends may do so also. If you give a seat to a senior citizen on a bus, your friends may do the same. As you engage in some of the activities suggested in this book, you will influence others. They may want to join you in your cause.

In addition to setting a good example, you can also help the world by writing songs, making posters, and telling stories that influence people's behavior. Kid power is most effective when lots of kids let their voices be heard. They write letters to newspapers. They influence people through personal appearances. They even give testimony at government hearings! If speaking up appeals to you, you'll be especially interested in Chapter Eight: "Uncle Sam Needs You!"

Create a plan of action

Once you have decided whom to help
and how to help, start to formulate a
plan of action. Do you have enough information to get started? You might want
to call or write to the agencies in this
book for information. Some organizations
will send you kits; some will send videos
or slides.

If you want to work with others, consider who those others might be: friends,
classmates, members of a club or Scout
troop, members of a volunteer organization that you would like to join. Whom-
ever you choose to work with, make sure
you share your ideas with these people
in an open way. Ask them for feedback.
Your co-workers may offer suggestions
that will make your plan more effective.
Don't ruin your efforts by being bossy!

Consider combining the efforts of a
group you belong to with a similar group
in another part of your community so
that you get to meet new kids. Working

together is a great way for people to make new friends. Often problems arise because different groups of people who have negative ideas about each other never get a chance to interact. By working together for a common cause, prejudices fade and strangers can become friends.

Do you need grown-ups to help you? Grown-ups can assist in many ways: by helping you make sure your plan is sensible and safe, by driving you places, by helping you construct things, by helping you phone and meet with businesspeople and government officials, and sometimes by supervising you. Your parents, teachers, members of the clergy, Scout leaders, coaches, senior citizens, and community leaders may be very willing to help.

> *Work is love made visible.*
> —Kahlil Gibran

Write down your plan of action. Your notes will help you keep track of dates, phone numbers, and other important details. Go over your plan to make sure you're organized and have what you need to put it into action. Check that people you are planning to help know what you are planning to do and when you are going to do it. Don't be like the family who took a homemade birthday dinner to a needy person—on the wrong day!

If you want your activity publicized, communicate dates and times clearly with newspapers and television stations in your area. Send them a letter or press release that explains the purpose of your activity. Tell them how excited you are. People like to know that kids are doing their share. Your actions, your words, and your power will be an inspiration to all.

I tell people that it's fun to help because you're thinking about the future. After I help, I feel really, really great, and I forget anything bad I've ever done. I feel like I've made a difference. Even small things, like going up and down your block and picking up litter, help, because if everyone did

it, we would have a cleaner Earth.
Sometimes all it takes is five minutes!
I always get excited when I do something
like that.

—Julia Carson, age 10
Mt. Kisco, New York

Helping
in
Your
Community

teachers, librarians, clergy, and
|||||||||||||||||||||||||||||||||| government officials in
your community have a great deal of
work to do. They can use your help! Volunteer to help them keep your community safe, clean, enjoyable, aware, and
beautiful. After all, a community is people living together, and a *good* community is people working together to make
life better for everyone. Kids all over
America have decided they want to help
improve their communities. Their ideas
and energy have made a big difference
for everyone around.

At school
* *set up a buddy system with
  kindergarten kids*

The fifth-grade students at Lakeview
School in Mahopac, New York, act as
buddies to kids in kindergarten. The
older kids help the younger ones by
showing them around the school in the
fall, helping them get on the right buses

in the afternoon, and playing games with them during recess. They also adopt a nearby pond together and make field trips to check the water quality and make lists of wild animals they see there. Ten-year-old Cathy Casti says, "I enjoy this program because I like working with kids. They are so cute. This is also fun because we get to do activities with them and go on trips and play."

We are always searching; I think that now we are at the point of finding.
—John Coltrane

● *build a better playground*
In many schools throughout the United States, budgets have been drastically cut, so students and parents are raising money and building new and better playgrounds themselves. They raise money with bake sales and school fairs, then construct playgrounds with climbing towers, tire swings, and tunnels. While the parents use hammers and nails, the kids baby-sit younger children and keep everyone supplied with lemon-

ade and cookies. One organization that provides information about how to build a playground is Jeff Olson, Inc., RD #2, Box 249, Marathon, NY 13803. (800) 345-6956.

● *re-create a prairie*
Middle school kids in Dayton, Ohio, are planting native American grasses in vacant lots and around their schools. Prairies once stretched from the Atlantic all the way to the Rocky Mountains, but today there are few prairies left. The students in Dayton are creating small prairies, and they are learning about plants such as blue big stem and Indian grass that covered the American prairie hundreds of years ago. If you want to plant a "mini-prairie" in your town, you can learn about native seeds and where to get them by sending for the booklet *Sources of Native Seeds and Plants* from Soil & Water Conservation Society, 7515 Northeast Ankeny Rd., Ankeny, IA 50021. The booklet costs $3 and lists sources for seeds in every state.

● *have a Spring Fling Week*
Students in Millbank, South Dakota, can't wait for spring! In early March they

get out their summer clothes and have a
baseball game and barbecue—even if
it's snowing! Their school also encour-
ages them to do good deeds that week.
Students think of ways to be kind to
someone else—they baby-sit for nothing,
pay their math teacher a compliment, or
visit someone who is lonely. On a piece
of paper, they write down every "kindness" they do along with their name,
and put the slips in a big box in the
school hallway. At the end of Spring
Fling Week, names are drawn from the
box and prizes are given to the lucky
winners. Many local businesses contribute prizes, because everyone in Millbank
gets spring fever and wants to celebrate!
You can organize a Spring Fling Week at
your school, too. Being kind to others is
a nice way to warm up.

- ***be a teacher's secret pal***
Teachers sometimes feel unappreciated
by their students. This idea—a good one
for a student council to sponsor—en-
ables students to cheer up teachers by
giving them secret presents throughout
the year. To start the project, count the
number of teachers and other staff you
want to include: aides, clerical workers,

maintenance workers, bus drivers, administrators, and so on. Then, ask for volunteer secret pals. You need a secret pal for every staff member you want to cheer up. During the year the secret pals leave little gifts and notes for their teachers. They might put a flower on a teacher's desk or a peppermint in a teacher's mailbox with a note that says, "You're worth a mint." The gifts may be small in cost and effort, but the positive effect on teachers is grand. At the end of the school year, have a party so the teachers can find out who their secret pals were—and can express their appreciation to them.

● *be a reading partner*
Volunteer to be a reading partner for younger children in your school. At Haldane School in Cold Spring, New York, third graders are reading partners for kindergartners. An entire class of third graders visits the kindergarten. Each third grader reads a book to his or her reading partner. Sometimes the third graders make books for their reading partners. The kindergartners learn to love books because the enthusiasm of the third graders for books is catching.

*I really think that when you're reading
to someone, it's like teaching
them to read and how to learn many things.
Maybe reading is the best way
for my reading partner to explore the world.
I feel like a grown-up when I read
to my reading partner.*
—Erica Maltese
Cold Spring, New York

• Harambee

Harambee is Swahili for "Let's all push together." In Poughkeepsie, New York, junior high kids in a program called Harambee are working as assistants to high school students who tutor young students in kindergarten through fifth grade. By working after school as tutor assistants, the Harambee kids are learning a skill as well as helping kids in their own community. Although you may be too young to tutor in an after-school program, you're not too young to be a tutor's assistant. Check with your teacher or principal about volunteering in after-school or summer tutoring programs for young kids.

- **recycle to read**

In Atlanta, Georgia, seventh-grade students helped second graders learn about recycling while they helped them read. Together, they collected discarded paper, cut it into 5" × 5" sheets, and stapled the sheets together to make note pads for teachers. With some of the paper, the seventh graders wrote and illustrated books that they read to the younger kids. This project helped beginning readers practice reading and learn about recycling. They also loved getting books they could keep.

- **donate a birthday book**

Ask your parents for a special book for your birthday. After reading it at home, donate the birthday book to the school library. The librarian can put a label in the front that says, "This birthday book is a gift from _____ on his/her _____ birthday."

- **help special children**

In Omaha, Nebraska, sixth grader Mike Gabb spends time with the younger students in his school who are in a special program for the physically challenged. He "sponsored" one of the kids in a

wheelchair at the school's Field Day,
and together they won a race! He also
helps teach these kids to play basketball
and catch. If your school, or a school
near you, has special programs for the
physically impaired, perhaps you can
volunteer to help in their sports program.

At the library
● *collect used books for a library book
  sale*
Many libraries have book sales to make
money. Kids can collect books from their
own homes and from neighbors to donate to the book sale. Sometimes kids
can help sort the books, put them on tables for the sale, and keep tables neat
during the sale.

- *be an animal!*

Fifth and sixth graders in Portland, Oregon, volunteered to help their community library with a project for preschoolers. The younger kids dictated letters to their "favorite animal." The volunteers did research at the library on the animals and then wrote back, answering questions about what they ate, where they lived, and even how they slept. They signed the letters with animal names such as "Molly the Muskrat" and "Ollie Owl" and decorated the letters with pictures. The younger kids were thrilled to hear from their favorite animals.

- *become an expert in children's books*

Even though you are too old for them yourself, read the children's books in your library until you know them well. Then, if your library doesn't have a children's librarian or if the children's librarian could use an assistant, volunteer to help kids select books that are on the right level for them.

- *stock the shelves*

Volunteer to spend one afternoon a week helping the children's librarian at school or at your community library. You can straighten up the shelves and put books back in their proper places.

Literature is my Utopia. Here I am not disenfranchised. No barrier of the senses shuts me out from the sweet, gracious discourse of my book friends.
—Helen Keller

● **make posters**
Zachary Potter of Tucson, Arizona, painted posters for classrooms and libraries to encourage people of all ages to read. The librarian was glad to have the posters and displayed them in the children's room and at the main desk.

● **deliver flowers**
Kirby Little of Lincoln, Nebraska, picked fresh flowers from his yard and took them to his local librarian in an inexpensive vase he bought at a tag sale. You can do this too. You can also use glass or plastic bottles for vases.

Community outdoor places
● **create a garden in an empty lot**
In New York City, kids who live near the Harlem and the Beth Abraham hospitals decided to make small abandoned plots

23

and the streets near the hospitals more attractive. With the help of knowledgeable adults from the Bronx Botanical Gardens and an organization called Green Thumb, they chose flowers and shrubs that grow well in New York City. Then they dug, cleaned, and watered the soil. Finally, they planted. After the plants started growing, the kids spent lots of time watering and weeding them. Some gardens have been named after the kids who made them! To start a community garden in your town, you will need the help of an adult supervisor such as your science teacher, Scout leader, or someone from the local garden club. For information on how to be involved in creating a community garden in your area, write: American Community Gardening Association, 325 Walnut St., Philadelphia, PA 19106.

Respect the plants.
—Park sign in Barcelona, Spain

● *build a bike path*
In Williston, Vermont, kids wanted a new bike path along an old railroad bed. Working with a teacher in their school,

they visited kids in nearby towns and made a plan to join the towns with a bike path. First they took a petition supporting their idea from door to door for people to sign. Then they took the petition to a town meeting and presented it to town officials. The kids can't build the path alone, so they are working to get adults in the community to help. Reed Albright, a ten-year-old who has attended town meetings and worked on a slide show to promote the idea, says, "It's fun working on this because it's great for kids—but the grown-ups want a bike path, too, so they can stay in shape." If you want to have a bike path, talk to your parents, teachers, Scout leaders, and town officials. Here's what a petition should look like:

Petition to Build a Bike Path

To: The Town Boards of Williston and Richmond

We the undersigned support the construction of a public bike path on the old railroad bed between Williston and Richmond. We agree to participate in building the path and to help with future maintenance.

Name ____ Address ____ Phone ____

• adopt a park

Do you have a neglected park in your town? In Frederick, Maryland, kids and adults decided to "adopt" a park that was in danger of being neglected because of budget cuts in park maintenance. The kids collected garbage and litter, raked leaves, and mowed the grass. They felt that this park was their own "big backyard" and wanted it to look good. They have a plan for working with state park officials and will send information if you write: Gambrill Volunteer Program, Gambrill State Park, 8602 Gambrill Park Rd., Frederick, MD 21702. (301) 473-8360.

*Let us look at the beauty of the little
corner where we live.
There are still many beautiful places on Earth
that we can protect and make more beautiful.
There are still many plants and
animals we can save from extinction.
That may help us survive.*

—Sophie Lakowski

● *clean up courts and fields*

Volunteer to clean up outdoor areas where people play and watch others play basketball, baseball, and other outdoor sports. If there are no trash cans, petition community officials to put some there. Make signs that ask people to use them.

● *adopt a scraggly garden*

Go on a garden tour of your community. Check out the schools, hospitals, libraries, and government offices. Do any of these places have a scraggly garden in need of care? Today, many officials lack funds to tend to their plantings. If you want to adopt a particular garden, write a letter stating your offer to the appropriate official. You, your family, or your organization may want to adopt a garden on a short- or long-term basis.

Community events
● *lend a hand at parades*

Parades are great celebrations for everyone, but there's always lots of work that has to be done before the big day. If you don't already belong to an organization that will be riding or marching in your town parade, ask your ambulance corps

or the volunteer fire department if they need help washing and waxing their trucks. If the parade is on a very hot day, you and some friends might be able to supply cold water and paper cups along the parade route.

● *help at auctions*
Sam Geer, age nine, of Garrison, New York, likes to help at charity auctions by "running the cards." When someone makes a successful bid for an item, he takes that person a card with the number of the item and the price so the buyer can get it later. Since Sam is smaller than an adult, it is easier for him to get through the crowd. He says, "It's hard work, but I like to do it because (a) it's fun working with my friends and (b) I like to help other people." Suggest being a helper to adults organizing a local charity auction. They may not have realized how valuable a smaller person can be.

● **come to the fair or block party**
Middle-grader Sophie Kolehmainen of
Chicago, Illinois, sold raffle tickets and
decorated children's faces with nontoxic
face paint to help raise money at a street
fair. Many local organizations have fairs
and block parties to raise money. You
can put together a list of annual fairs,
festivals, and block parties in your area.
Such events are usually hosted by art
centers, libraries, churches, neighborhood associations, and hospitals. You
can call these organizations and find out
when and where their fairs will be and
who is organizing the events. Choose a
fair that interests you, and ask if the or-
ganizer could use your help.

*We should all be concerned about the future
because we will have to spend
the rest of our lives there.*
—Charles F. Kettering

● **give away your extra day**
In Houston, Texas, kids and their families
find ways to celebrate February 29—the
extra day that comes every fourth year,
or leap year—by volunteering to do special service in their community. Walter
Black, director of the Volunteer Center in

29

Houston, says, "Every friendly deed makes the world a little friendlier." Kids collect food for the Houston Food Bank, donate good used clothes to a shelter, weed community gardens, or visit nursing homes. Of course, these kids don't wait four years before they do another good deed. Because helping others is so satisfying, they find ways to help throughout the year. Check the white pages in your telephone book for a volunteer center in your community. These centers will tell you about volunteer opportunities in your area.

He that brings sunshine into the lives of others cannot keep it from himself.
—Anonymous

People
Who
Help
People

today, many people in America are ▐▟▊▊▊▊▊▊▊▊▊▊▊▊▊ homeless. Some are older people. Some are whole families—mothers, fathers, and kids. Some have psychological problems. All are poor. Homeless people may go to temporary shelters for a place to sleep, some warm food, or help in finding a permanent home. By volunteering to work in such shelters, by donating food and clothing to them, or by raising money for homeless people, you can help.

Others besides the homeless need you, too. People who have been abused or threatened go to shelters where they are safe. At the shelter, they may need clothes, books, and toys—cheerful things to help them through hard times. Older people who live alone also may need help. You can go shopping for them. You can take a walk with them or simply keep them company.

A popular song in the 1970s included the line "People who need people are the luckiest people in the world." A better

line might be, "People who *help* people
are the luckiest people in the world."
You can be one of them.

Helping the homeless
- *help build or renovate a home for the homeless*

In Omaha, Nebraska, thirteen-year-old
Jeff Williamson and some of his friends
volunteered to help renovate an old
house so it could be used by a homeless
family. They spent hours hauling out old
plaster and sweeping up plaster dust! It
was hard work, but when the house was
ready for the new family they felt satis-
fied with their work. They were part of a
team who volunteered to help Habitat for
Humanity. To find out if you can help
build or renovate homes for the homeless, write to: Habitat for Humanity, 121
Habitat St., Americus, GA 31709-3498.
(912) 924-6935.

- *make bread trips*

A mother in Berkeley, California, saw an
old man rummaging through a trash bin
searching for food. She thought of all the
good food that restaurants, schools, and
stores throw away. She decided to collect this food and give it to hungry peo-

ple. Her program, called Daily Bread, now helps provide fresh food to many people. Many other people, including kids, help out. Sixth graders in San Francisco, California, regularly collect all the uneaten fresh fruit and unopened milk cartons from their school cafeteria and take these items to a shelter. A Girl Scout troop went door to door and collected canned goods, which were taken to a soup kitchen. Another group of kids collected extra apples, pears, and peaches from their backyard fruit trees and donated them. Still others volunteered to work in the Daily Bread community garden, which was planted to grow food for the hungry. Daily Bread feeds people without raising money. Because everyone shares and works together, the organization doesn't even need a budget. For more information, write to: Carolyn North, Daily Bread, 2447 Prince St., Berkeley, CA 94705. (510) 848-3522.

The Loaf

I ate my bread
And was hungry still;
I sipped my cup
And yet my throat was dry;
I asked for larger loaf and when denied
I wept because I could not have my fill.
And then I gave
My last small precious crumb to one, alone,
Who hungered more than I;
And, lo,
The loaves that heaped upon my board
Reached the sky.

—Berenice M. Rice

● **make some MAD money**
Kids at the Christopher Wren School in
Queens, New York, are "mad" for money.
MAD stands for "Make a Difference," and
these students are making a difference
by collecting cans everywhere they find
them, redeeming them, and then donating the money to an organization for the
homeless. They also make posters about
MAD and stand outside neighborhood
supermarkets to explain further. Many
people are glad to give their returnable
bottles to these kids when they see that
their money will go to help the homeless.

- *start a "milk for kids" project*

With an adult to help you, you can ask your local grocery store to set up a "milk for kids" project. Here's how it works: Coupons are placed near the check-out stations in grocery stores. Shoppers are invited to pay for an extra carton of milk. When they do, a coupon is stamped and placed in a collection box. On a regular basis, a volunteer exchanges the coupons for fresh milk and delivers the milk to an agency that distributes free food.

To do this you need to ask the store manager to help, make posters explaining how to buy coupons, find a shelter that needs the milk, and ask an adult to help deliver the milk. Lots of effort, but it can work! Daily Bread (see page 34) will send you detailed information and a sample coupon if you want to try this.

Milk for Children Who Need It

Please make *milk* available to *under-nourished children* in Berkeley and Oakland:

1. Pay 90¢ to *reserve* a half-gallon of milk when you check out at the Co-op.

2. Tear off the coupon below. Checker will stamp it and keep it.

3. Donation is tax-deductible; keep upper portion for your records.

4. Daily Bread volunteers will redeem your stamped coupons for milk, and deliver the milk to local centers for free distribution to needy children.

Thank you.

New volunteers welcome!
- one hour per week -
call Daily Bread, 848-3522.

------------TEAR OFF------------

A half-gallon of milk for a needy family with children

Co-op
Stamp
Here

Code 1451   90¢ MILK
Daily Bread   COUPON

*I expect to pass through this world
but once; any good thing therefore that
I can do, or any kindness that I can
show to any fellow creature, let me do
it now; let me not defer or neglect it,
for I shall not pass this way again.*
—Attributed to Stephen Grellet

Family sanctuaries

A family sanctuary is a place where people can go if they have been physically abused. At the sanctuary they are safe from physical harm while steps are taken to protect them. If you'd like to help out at a sanctuary near you, call the United Way—it's listed in the white pages of your phone book. The United Way is a group of charitable organizations that work together to raise money, find volunteers, and tell people where to get help.

● *pack treat bags for kids in sanctuaries*
Children who have gone with a parent to a family sanctuary need something to cheer them up. You can put together treat bags to greet them. In the bags, put

37

some crayons, coloring books, a pack of gum, candy, and simple, inexpensive games. People who work in these shelters are very busy and may not be able to make things like these treat bags available for kids. *You* know what kids like and what will make them feel better. Pack things in the bag that you would want to receive. You may need to raise funds in order to purchase them (see Chapter Nine), or you might find local stores willing to donate supplies. You can make different kinds of bags for different age groups. Label the ages on the bags.

Love is not like a bag of sugar.
You can't lose it by giving it away.
—Elizabeth McCormack

• *comfort with cookies*
Call a shelter and say you want to help someone celebrate a birthday or a special occasion. Let the shelter suggest a day and time. Ask what you can bring: balloons, decorations, game ideas, and perhaps even a homebaked birthday cake or cupcakes.

Older friends

● adopt a grandparent

In New York City, kids have joined a group called Friendly Visiting. When they join, they list their hobbies and interests. They are then paired with older people who have similar interests. The kids visit their older friends or walk with them to a nearby coffee shop for a cup of tea. Sometimes the kids push their friends' carts in grocery stores. Older people in large cities are sometimes lonely. They may also feel like targets for purse snatchers, but with their younger friends, they feel safe. Find out more by writing: Friendly Visiting, Attn: Cynthia Maurer, 401 Lafayette St., New York, NY 10003-7802.

It's very thrilling to help someone younger, older, or the same age as I am.
— Maria D'Amato
Cold Spring, New York

● visit the elderly in hospitals and nursing homes

In West Des Moines, Iowa, middle school students participate in the I CARE program. After school, seventh and eighth graders walk to a nearby nursing home, where many of the older people need to use wheelchairs. The kids wheel the residents into the dining room for their evening meal and sometimes help them cut their meat or get extra cups of juice. The students also like to bring treats with them, such as homemade cookies and cupcakes. After dinner, they sometimes read to the older people from a favorite book or the newspaper. If you want to volunteer to help in an elder care facility, call your local United Way for the name of one near you. When you call the facility, tell them your age and interests.

The Golden Rule:
Do unto others as you would have them
do unto you.

● *tape-record stories*
Ask your grandparents to tell you tales about their childhood, and record them on your tape recorder. They will enjoy the project and the knowledge that someday their great-grandchildren might hear the stories! Play the stories back for them on their birthdays!

You give but little when you
give of your possessions. It is when you
give of yourself that you truly give.
> —Kahlil Gibran

● **tell someone you care**
Ten-year-old Virginia Calhoun, from
Charlotte, North Carolina, stood up in
front of all the people gathered for her
grandmother's seventy-fifth birthday
party and said she loved her grandmother because she was always there
for her when she felt sad or was hurt.
Virginia's grandmother said it was the
best birthday present of all.

● **celebrate a birthday with an older**
  person
A family in Berkeley, California, learned
that a very old woman who lived in a
nearby nursing home rarely had visitors.
They found out when her birthday was
and brought cake, candles, and ice
cream. She loved hearing them sing
"Happy Birthday" to her and enjoyed her
birthday celebration. To find nursing
homes in your area, look in the yellow
pages or call the United Way.

41

- **read to, listen to, and talk to an older person**

At the Louis Armstrong Middle School in Queens, New York, seventh-grade students started the Partners Program, during which they made weekly visits to the Franklin Nursing Home. Before they went, their teacher helped them understand what it is like to be visually and physically impaired. The volunteers prepared themselves by discussing the process of aging. At their weekly visits to the nursing home, the children worked on oral history projects, helped make picture frames and plant holders, gave parties, and even worked in the kitchen. A national organization that can help you start a similar project or can suggest ideas for many other volunteer projects is: National Center for Service and Learning in Early Adolescence, CASE/CUNY, 25 W. 43rd St., Room 612, New York, NY 10036. (212) 642-2947.

I hear and I forget
I see and I remember
I do and I understand.
　　　　—Chinese proverb

● *have a senior citizen prom*
Each year high school students in East
Hartford, Connecticut, invite the senior
citizens in their town to a special prom.
Girls who volunteer wear fancy dresses;
boys who volunteer wear tuxedos donated by a rental store. Two boys meet
each arriving lady and escort her to the
dance floor. The girls escort the gentle-
men. The dance floor, in the cafeteria, is
decorated beautifully for the occasion.
The students serve the senior citizens a
spaghetti dinner and raffle off many
prizes donated by townspeople. Afterward, two bands take turns playing. The
bands are paid for with the $1 admission
collected from the seniors. Invitations go
out early so that RSVPs can be collected
in time to plan the special event. Some
years the seniors have given each other

dancing lessons before the big night. Though this event has been put on by high school students, it could also be done by junior high students with parents and teachers to help.

I had more fun at the senior citizen prom than I had at the junior prom!
—Mark Hope,
President of the senior class
East Hartford High School

Help fight illiteracy

Imagine you are a new kid in school. You are nervous and shy. A woman in the office smiles at you and says, "You will be in Ms. Jones's class. Just go down this hall and find her name on the door." You walk down the hall. There are doors on both sides with writing on them. But you don't know which one says "Ms. Jones" because *you cannot read!*

Many adults in America could not find Ms. Jones's room because they are illiterate. They are also nervous and shy when they are with people who expect them to read. As many as one out of every five adults cannot read well enough to fill out a job application.

● *help adults read*

In Missouri, students all over the state
participate in KHAR—Kids Helping
Adults Read. Kids collect pledges (usually one cent per page) from friends,
family, and neighbors based on the
number of pages they read during their
summer break. At the end of the summer, they collect the pledges and donate
their earnings to an organization that
sponsors reading programs for illiterate
adults. If you want to start a KHAR program in your state, write to: LIFT—Missouri, 300 S. Broadway, St. Louis, MO
63102. (314) 421-1970. LIFT (Literacy In-
vestment for Tomorrow) will send you
detailed information on how KHAR
works. You will need an organization
that promotes adult literacy to sponsor
you. A local chapter of Literacy Volunteers of America (check the white pages)
might help.

Hide not your talents,
they for use were made.
What's a Sun-dial in the Shade?
—Benjamin Franklin

- *give books for babies*
Give your old baby books to hospitals
and clinics for new mothers and babies.
Donate used magazines with colorful
pictures to clinics or health care centers.

Helping
Out at
Holiday
Time

holidays are an ideal time to help people in need. If everyone would take a little time to reach out during holidays, the world would be a much happier place. You can do some of the projects in this chapter by yourself or with friends. Some of them are perfect for families to do together. Since families often make a point of being together at holiday time, it can be easy for them to arrange to work together, too. Many people feel that the helpful projects they share at holiday time make their holidays happier and more meaningful. Indeed, they feel that their family has been enriched by acting upon the concept that we are all members of the "human family."

When indeed shall we learn that we are
all related one to the other,
that we are all members of one body?
—Helen Keller

Helping hands at Halloween

- *make sure your "loot bag" has a UNICEF box*

Collect money at Halloween for UNICEF (United Nations International Children's Fund). UNICEF works in 128 countries to help educate and vaccinate millions of children each year. The organization also helps villages dig water wells and distribute medicines, dietary supplements, and emergency food. Its goal is to bring good health and hope for the future to the children of developing nations. You can get your UNICEF boxes at your school, or write to: U.S. Committee for UNICEF, 333 E. 38th St., New York, NY 10016.

- *haunt a house for your favorite charity*

In Omaha, Nebraska, Mike Gabb and his friends are monstrous on Halloween! To raise money for school athletic equipment, the sixth graders organized a haunted house. They dressed up in scary outfits and gathered in an old house owned by neighbors. They advertised their haunted house and charged trick-or-treaters $1 to walk through it. Witches cackled, monsters jumped out of closets, and "fortune tellers" predicted the future. Some adults even walked through the

49

haunted house for thrills! Mike and his
friends made more than $500 and en-
joyed scaring everyone. If you know
someone with an old house who would
like to help you raise money for a favorite cause, you and your friends can create a haunted house too. Ghouls, ghosts,
and witches are welcome!

● *trick-or-treat so others can eat!*
An organization in Virginia that helps
the homeless will tell you how to trick-
or-treat for canned food instead of just
candy. You will need a driver to carry
and then deliver all the food you collect.
Trick-or-treaters have learned that even
when they are collecting extra cans of
food for the homeless, there is still
plenty of candy. When kids work together on Halloween night, they often
have a party afterward to see how many

cans of tuna, jars of peanut butter, or packages of dried soup they've collected. To get a packet of information explaining how to set up this Halloween project, write: People Helping People, P.O. Box 551, Dahlgren, VA 22448. (703) 663-2230.

If I can stop one Heart from breaking
I shall not live in vain
If I can ease one Life the Aching
Or cool one Pain
Or help one fainting Robin
Unto his Nest again
I shall not live in Vain.
—Emily Dickinson

● *party for muscular dystrophy*
The Muscular Dystrophy Association gives Halloween parties for kids with muscular dystrophy. They like to have families attend and help make their parties a success. Call your local MDA chapter to find out if parties are given in your area and how you can help. Ask them for information about how muscular dystrophy affects people so you will be prepared to talk to and assist people with this disease at the party.

Love sought is good,
but giv'n unsought is better.
—William Shakespeare

Helping hands at Thanksgiving
● *cook a holiday meal for the homeless*
In Urbana, Illinois, one family cooked a complete Thanksgiving dinner for twenty people who were living in a nearby shelter. The family planned the meal, went shopping together the day before, and got up at 5:00 A.M. on Thanksgiving morning to get everything ready. They delivered three roasted turkeys, three gallons of peas, and four gallons of mashed potatoes (wrapped in foil and towels to keep them warm) to the shelter, where they served a real home-cooked meal complete with salad, rolls, and drinks. The people in the shelter would have had frozen dinners if this family had not worked so hard.

If you want to cook a meal for a needy family or shelter, talk to your religious leader or call a shelter in your city or town. Make sure the shelter or family can take your meal. Be sure they know exactly what day and time you will deliver it.

- **help prepare Thanksgiving food baskets for a nearby food pantry**

Twelve-year-old Carston Vogel of Honolulu, Hawaii, gets up early once a month to take his food package to a nearby food pantry on his way to school. He likes to include extra goodies with the rice, soup, and fresh fruit that he and his mother pack. He loves M&M's, so he figures homeless people do too! At Thanksgiving, he and other students from his school go to the food pantry to divide up the donated cans of pumpkin and mincemeat, fresh oranges, packaged stuffing, yams, and cranberries into individual family food baskets. He says, "At the first Thanksgiving, Indians shared their food with the Pilgrims . . . so it's a Thanksgiving tradition to share food."

A food pantry is a place that distributes food to people who don't have enough money to buy it in stores. Food pantries sometimes need help dividing donated food into family baskets. To find food pantries near you, call the United Way—it's listed in the white pages of your phone book.

Not what we give, but what we share—
For the gift without the giver is bare.
—James Russell Lowell

Helping hands at Christmas and Hanukkah

● *go caroling with friends*

Good places to go caroling are hospitals and nursing homes. Call the places beforehand to find out when is the best time to visit. Have songbooks or the words to songs printed on sheets so that everyone knows what to sing. If possible, have someone play an instrument, such as a guitar or portable keyboard, to accompany the carolers.

● *have a Christmas/Hanukkah volleyball tournament*

Instead of charging money for admission, ask that fans donate a new toy or book for a child. Have volunteers collect the toys as people come in. Volleyball players can be kids, grown-ups, or both. Ask school physical education teachers to referee.

● **deck the halls**
Volunteer to help put up holiday decorations in a local nursing home, children's hospital, or shelter for the homeless. To find out about shelters in your area, call the United Way.

● **be a Santa for a homeless child**
A family in Nashville, Tennessee, decided that instead of giving each other gifts, they would pool all the money they would have spent and buy new toys for homeless children. There were still *plenty* of gifts under their tree from friends, grandparents, and other family members, and they had the special gift of knowing they had made some children very happy. There are many organizations that collect new toys for homeless kids at Christmastime. Watch for notices in your local paper or call the Salvation Army in your town.

I think we should help other people
who are less fortunate than us because we
would not want to be in their shoes
with no gifts for this special holiday
of love and peace.

—Matt Heiser, age 11
Mahopac, New York

55

- **wrap presents that have been collected for poor families**

Many groups collect toys for the poor. Find out who does that in your area by calling churches, the police or sheriff's office, and social service organizations. Call and say that you'd like to volunteer to wrap the presents. You might ask local merchants to donate wrapping paper for the cause.

- **have a Mexican (or Brazilian or Polish) Christmas exchange party**

A Methodist church in Virginia has a special relationship with a church in Mexico. Church members donate toys, toiletries, and other gifts that the kids wrap at a special Mexican Christmas party on the first Sunday in December. The church makes a video of the party and sends it with the boxes of presents to Mexico. The Mexican church video-tapes *its* party as the recipients open their gifts and celebrate Christmas.

Once I gave my Christmas money
to the poor because it made me feel better.
It was forty dollars. I only did that once,
but it was worth it.

—David Bates, age 12
Chicago, Illinois

Run,
Rock,
and Rap
for
Health

people all over the world are working together to find the cures for life-threatening diseases such as cancer, muscular dystrophy, AIDS, and multiple sclerosis. Doctors, scientists, and health care workers are all doing their part—but kids can help too! Although some health organizations and most hospitals require that volunteers be at least sixteen, many others welcome kids' help with office work or at special parties for patients.

The best way (and sometimes the most fun way) to help health causes is to raise money for them. You can do this in all kinds of ways: by running, swimming, dancing, and even rocking in a rocking chair! You can work with friends in an event you sponsor yourselves, or you can participate in an event sponsored by a health organization. If you want to help a health organization, call the office nearest your home for information. To find local chapters of national health organizations, call the United Way.

*To leave the world a bit better,
whether by a healthy child, a garden
patch, or a redeemed social condition;
to know even one life has breathed
easier because you have lived.
This is to have succeeded.*
—Ralph Waldo Emerson

Run or help others run

● *run—or set up a pit stop for runners*
Ronald McDonald Houses are places
where people can stay while a family
member is being treated in a nearby
hospital. To raise money, one Ronald
McDonald House sponsored a fun run in
Morgantown, West Virginia, in which
people donated $12 to enter a five-mile
run and got a T-shirt. Some kids decided
to help by setting up a pit stop for runners halfway through the race. At the pit
stop they had ice, pitchers of water, and
small paper cups. They provided thirsty
runners with a drink to help them run on
a hot day. Tyler Smith, who helped at
the pit stop, said, "It was more fun helping others complete the race than running it myself. I just hope when I decide
to run, someone else has a pit stop for me!"

59

The English poet John Milton once wrote: "They also serve who only stand and wait." By standing and waiting with cool drinks, these kids helped make the day a great success. Call your local Ronald McDonald House if you want to help in a fun run.

● *clown around at a bike-a-thon*
At bike-a-thons kids and adults ride their bikes to raise money. The American Diabetes Association sponsors its own special bike-a-thons to raise money for diabetes research. The bike-a-thons are called Tour de Cure and take place in May in cities throughout the United States. To make this event more fun for everyone, in 1991 kids in Boston dressed up like clowns and joined the "tour." They also ran a tricycle mini-tour for the very young kids. The clowns helped the little kids get started and cheered for

them. The younger kids loved seeing the
clowns waving them to the finish line.
To find out about the Tour de Cure or a
bike-a-thon near you, write: American
Diabetes Association, 1660 Duke St., Alexandria, VA 22314. (800) 232-3472.

● *participate in the Special Olympics*
   Parade of Athletes
The Special Olympics, which were be-
gun by the Joseph P. Kennedy, Jr., Foundation, are competitive games and races
for people who are mentally challenged.
If there are Special Olympics events in
your community, consult the organizers
to see how you might help. Your Scout
troop could offer to be the color guard
(flag bearers) for the opening ceremo-
nies. You also might be able to escort
participants during the parade or make
special decorations. Each state has its
own events and requirements for partici-
pation. The Special Olympics organization in your state will be listed as the
(State name) Special Olympics in the
white pages of your phone book.

● *take a walk for babies' health*
On the last Sunday in April, you can
take a walk to support the March of

61

Dimes campaign for healthier babies. The March of Dimes WalkAmerica is held every year, nationwide, to raise money for research into ways to prevent birth defects and infant mortality. The March of Dimes also works with parents to teach them how to have healthier babies. Ask your friends, parents, and neighbors to sponsor you, and see if you can go the whole distance—30 kilometers (19 miles)! You might also be able to help organize a mini-walk for younger kids. To find out more, write: March of Dimes/ WalkAmerica, 233 Park Ave. South, New York, NY 10013. (212) 353-8353.

Swim for others
● *swim laps at summer camp*
At the Breeze Mont Camp in Armonk, New York, campers got pledges from family and friends for laps they swam during the summer. Every lap they swam earned money for Friends of Karen, an organization that helps families with children who have life-threatening diseases. The campers swam enough laps to raise $14,000! A motto at Friends of Karen is "Children helping children," and kids all over the United States have helped each other through this organization. Although Friends of Karen has no

national office, you can check to see if there is a chapter near you by looking in the white pages of your phone book.

Rock, roll, and rap

• *organize a rock-a-thon*

Kids sitting around in rocking chairs? You bet! Parents and grandparents pledged money for every half hour kids would sit and rock! The kids didn't do it all at once, but over a month they spent enough time rocking to raise lots of money for the Multiple Sclerosis Society. To organize a rock-a-thon or participate in the society's annual walkathon, call the chapter nearest you. The society is listed in the white pages of your phone book.

• *roll up lucky money*

Is there a mall near you that has a fountain? Are the coins from the fountain donated to a local charity? Did you ever wonder what that charity did with all those wet pennies and nickels? Often, the coins are sent to the charity in large barrels and need to be wrapped up before they can be deposited in a bank. Find out which charity the mall sends their lucky fountain coins to. Call the charity to see if you can help wrap the coins.

● *rap against drugs*
Eighth graders in Pine Bluff, Arkansas, rap to show younger elementary school kids how to have a good time without getting into drugs. With their school counselor, these kids developed a program of skits and rap music that they perform in the local elementary schools. They call their group IMPRES—Information Makes Prevention Realistic and Effective. They show kids how to improve their self-esteem and develop a positive self-image. After the group members perform, they stay and have lunch with the younger kids so they can talk to them individually and encourage them to stay away from drugs and alcohol.

*Nothing great was ever achieved
without enthusiasm.*
—Ralph Waldo Emerson

Phone, compute—and sew!
- *be computer friendly*

Some chapters of the American Cancer
Society allow kids to help enter data on
their computer systems. Since kids are
sometimes more comfortable with computers than many of the older volunteers,
kids work the computers and teach others how. They also stuff envelopes, lick
stamps, and help file papers. Call your
local American Cancer Society and see if
they need someone who is computer
friendly.

- *get in touch*

At Muscular Dystrophy Association offices, kids participate in an In Touch
program. They telephone people who
have the disease and ask them if they
need anything special. Often they just
talk with them for a while. If a person
needs special transportation or someone
to visit, the kids tell the adults in the office. Since many people with muscular
dystrophy are homebound, they look for-
ward to talking with the kids. You can
find out more by writing: Muscular Dystrophy Association, 3561 E. Sunrise Dr.,
Tucson, AZ 85718, or calling your local
chapter.

• take a walk for AIDS research

To find a cure for AIDS and to stop the spread of the disease, a lot of money is needed for research. In New York City, kids, parents, and friends walk ten kilometers through Central Park to raise money for AIDS research. As in other walkathons, the walkers ask people to sponsor them; sponsors pay a certain amount of money for every mile that's walked. The walkers have fun because lots of people participate. Some people dress up, some bring guitars for singing. Everyone feels they are helping a very important cause. AIDS walks take place in many cities and are sponsored by various organizations. To participate in an AIDS walk, keep an eye out in your local paper for notice of one. Or call the Centers for Disease Control (CDC) National AIDS Hotline at (800) 342-AIDS for information on how to find an organization in your area that is concerned with AIDS.

> *My father encouraged me to do the walk because my godfather had AIDS. And when I did, I was proud that I raised $200 and that I walked the whole six miles.*
> —Robert O'Connor, 12

*I liked it because it made me
remember my godfather, and it almost
felt as if I was walking with him.*
—Edward O'Connor, 8

- **make a memorial panel for the NAMES
  Project AIDS Memorial Quilt**

If you want to remember a friend who
has died of AIDS or if you just want to
help fight the disease, your family can
have a quilting bee to make a quilt
panel for the NAMES Project Quilt. Your
family panel can be a part of the quilt,
which now has more than six thousand
panels! The memorial quilt is displayed
in cities throughout America. To learn
how you can make a panel, write or call
the NAMES Project Foundation, 2362 Market St., San Francisco, CA 94114. (415)

863-5511. They will send you instructions on how to sew a panel and provide you with the address of the closest chapter to you.

Animals
Who
Need
You

when kids all over America learned that dolphins were being killed because they were caught and trapped in tuna drift nets, they took action. They got their parents to stop buying tuna, wrote to political leaders, and raised money for organizations trying to stop the use of drift nets by fishermen. Even though there was no single national organization that brought these efforts together, many kids working together were able to stop the use of drift nets and to save hundreds of thousands of dolphins. Adults saw how much power kids can have and how much difference kid power can make. Today there are many worldwide organizations that help kids save animals. These organizations welcome donations and want to hear kids' ideas for saving endangered animals. Send them your suggestions, as well as artwork, short stories, and poems. Your concern for animals really makes a difference!

Endangered species

- *give a video pizza party (no tuna) for dolphins*

Order the video *Where Have All the Dolphins Gone?* from the Save the Dolphins Project, and invite your friends and neighbors to see it. The video shows how dolphins have been caught in tuna nets and what is being done to save them. Although many dolphins have been saved, there is still more work to be done. After you've seen the video together, discuss how you can help. To order a video, send $11 (you can keep the video for a month) to Save the Dolphins Project, Earth Island Institute, 300 Broadway, Suite 28, San Francisco, CA 94133-3312. (415) 788-3666.

- *make your school lunchroom "dolphin-safe"*

Students in West Chester, Pennsylvania, wanted to make sure the tuna being served in school was dolphin-safe. With the assistance of their teacher and with information supplied by the Save the Dolphins Project, they circulated a petition, and wrote to and met with the school's food supplier, the president of Mitsui Foods, Inc. (a tuna canner), and their U.S. representative. As a result,

71

their school does not buy tuna caught by fishermen who use drift nets.

• start a wolf club
Many people fear wolves and want them killed. But kids in the sixth grade at Dogwood Elementary School in Smithtown, New York, believe that wolves have a right to live. They "adopted" (sent money to help feed and care for) a wolf from Wolf Haven, a facility in Washington State that protects captured wolves. His name is Lucan, and they made him their school mascot. The students also submitted artwork about wolves to the Imagine Yellowstone Art Exhibit and wrote letters to their representatives and the governor of Alaska about protecting wolves. Wildlife experts even brought two wolves to visit their school! For their hard work on behalf of wolves, President

Bush commended the Dogwood Elementary School for outstanding achievement in environmental protection services. To find out how your school can adopt a wolf, write: Wolf Haven International, 3111 Offut Lake Rd., Tenino, WA 98589. (800) 448-WOLF. To learn more about wolves, write International Wolf Center, c/o Vermilion Community College, 1900 E. Camp St., Ely, MN 55731. (800) 475-6666.

Behold the turtle, he makes progress only when he sticks his neck out.
—Sign on the office wall of J. B. Conant, former president of Harvard University

● *make turtle cards*

Many Olive Ridley sea turtles are being killed so their skin can be used to make expensive shoes. Other sea turtles are killed and stuffed for wall decorations. If these practices continue, there will be no more sea turtles. Students in Tarzana, California, decided to help stop the slaughter. They made cards with pictures of the turtles on them to create interest and raised money by doing chores and having a sale at which everything cost less than a dollar. The students raised $141.62, which they sent to the Sea Turtle Restoration Project, Earth Island Institute, 300 Broadway, Suite 28, San Francisco, CA 94133-3312. (415) 788-3666. Write or call for a packet of information and a video about the sea turtles.

● *give a mustang free range*
You can help buy an acre of rangeland for wild mustangs in South Dakota. There are over 1,600 mustangs that need free range to roam and forage for food. For $100 you can save an acre in a special private sanctuary as well as help feed and care for the herd. If you travel to South Dakota, you can see the horses for yourself—there are free tours of the sanctuary. To find out how to help the American mustangs, write: The Institute of Range and the American Mustang (IRAM), Box 998, Hot Springs, SD 57747. (800) 252-6652.

We are part of the Earth
And the Earth is a part of us.
The fragrant flowers are our sisters,
The reindeer, the horse,
The great eagle our brothers.
　　　　　　　　　　—Chief Seattle

● *help protect whale habitats*
Whales travel great distances—from
Baja California to the Bering Sea in
Alaska on the west coast of North America, and from the Caribbean to New England on the east coast. Whale infants
are born in the south and travel north
with their mothers to nurse and grow in
northern waters in summertime. This
"loop" the whales travel must be pro-
tected from whaling (whale hunting), debris, and offshore oil drilling. The Center
for Marine Conservation works to protect
the whales' feeding and nursing waters
by research, lobbying, and creating public awareness. The center will send you
information about whales, tell you how
to write letters to congressional leaders
supporting the moratorium on killing
whales, and help you prepare a whale
project for your classroom. Write: Center
for Marine Conservation, 1725 DeSales
St. NW, Suite 500, Washington, DC. (202)
429-5609.

You can also adopt a Pacific hump-
back whale for $25 and get an official
certificate and a color photograph of
your whale's tail flukes. To adopt a
whale and find out more about Pacific
whales, write: Pacific Whale Foundation,
101 N. Kihei Rd., Kihei, HI 96753. (800)
WHALE-11.

• *save elephants and rhinos*

Kids in New York have started a letter-writing campaign to Korea to stop the killing of elephants and rhinos for the ivory in their tusks. Since most of the ivory is bought by Koreans, the letters are sent to the Korean ambassador at the United Nations. As part of the project, the kids, accompanied by TV camera crews, visited the zoo to see elephants and rhinos. Their concerns were nationally televised by CNBC-TV's *Home and Family* show. If you want to help, write: KiDS S.T.O.P., P.O. Box 471, Forest Hills, NY 11375. Send a self-addressed, stamped envelope for a reply.

• *write for wildlife*

There are many people and organizations to whom you can write about endangered species. Before you write, however, find out facts about the animals you want to save and why they are being killed. You need to do research at school and at the library. For a pamphlet that explains the dos and don'ts of writing to government officials, big businesses, and other organizations, write: Defenders of Wildlife, 1244 19th St. NW, Washington, DC 20036. (202) 659-9510.

Animals near you

● *get WIZE about zoo animals*

Ask your teacher to get the WIZE (Wildlife Inquiry Through Zoo Education) packet from the Bronx Zoo for your class. This packet of educational materials will help you understand what zoos do and tell you how you can participate in your own local zoo. Write: Don Lisowy, Project WIZE, Bronx Zoo Education Dept., Bronx, NY 10460.

● *adopt an animal in the zoo*

Zoos can use your help in providing food and shelter for animals. One thing you can do is adopt an animal by sending money to your zoo. You might be able to raise money by starting a lion club or an elephant club and sending the dues regularly to the zoo. Your club can make visits and see how "your" animals are doing and perhaps make friends with the caretaker. Some zoos use students to help with tours or to help take care of zoo grounds. Each zoo has its own needs and requirements for volunteers, so if you want to help, call your local zoo for information.

● *help with abandoned animals*

Most communities have organizations such as the ASPCA (American Society for

the Prevention of Cruelty to Animals) to provide shelter for abandoned animals. Larger animal shelters often sponsor events such as "dog walks" to raise money. A dog walk is similar to a walk-athon, except you take your dog with you! You get pledges for each mile you walk with your dog. Dog walks can be held in city parks (there's an annual one in Central Park in New York City) or even in neighborhoods. You can help animal shelters by participating in such fund-raising events. Sometimes you can even work in a shelter feeding or caring for animals. Usually there is an age requirement (over eighteen) to actually work with the animals, but each shelter is different. To find a list of animal shelters in your area, look in the yellow pages under "Animal shelters."

● *ask your teacher to go WILD*
Imagine your own school playground as
a place where both kids and wild animals such as raccoons and muskrats can
live. Now imagine that your idea's come
true—because it can. Project WILD will
send information to schools and train
teachers so you can work together to
share your habitat with wild animals.
Ask your teacher to write: Project WILD,
P.O. Box 18060, Boulder, CO 80308. (303)
444-2390.

If you have hard work to do,
do it now.
Today the skies are clear and blue
tomorrow clouds may come in view,
yesterday is not for you;
do it now.
—Charles R. Skinner

Bringing birds back
● *join a bird team*
Every year at Christmastime, the Audubon Society sponsors bird counts. Teams
of "birders" go out early in the morning
and count the birds they see. They re-

ceive previously pledged donations for each species. This money is donated to help preserve local bird habitats. You could be a "spotter"—you spot a bird, and the birder will identify it. An extra pair of eyes is always useful during the Christmas bird count, and you'll learn to identify birds while you help. To learn about this and other Audubon activities, write: National Audubon Society, Educational Division, 950 Third Ave., New York, NY 10022.

● *build custom birdhouses*
Students in Silver City, New Mexico, worked with their local Audubon Society representative, a naturalist from the U.S. Forest Service, and their industrial arts teacher to build special birdhouses for bluebirds. Bluebirds are territorial and won't build their nests near other bluebirds. So the kids put the houses up along trails in the Gila National Forest, making sure they were at least a half-mile apart. Later, they loved taking walks along the trails to see how their bluebird families were doing. Find out what kinds of houses different birds look for and how to build them. Consult

books in your public library or local nature centers. Books published by the National Audubon Society will be especially helpful.

● *build a sanctuary—it's for the birds!*
The school grounds of Yonkers School 29 have been certified as an urban wildlife sanctuary because the students have worked there to plant "bird friendly" trees such as hawthorn and crab apple. They have built special winter bird feeders and bird water fountains and made sure there were evergreen trees and shrubs where birds could find shelter in the wintertime. To learn how your school can create a bird sanctuary, write: National Institute for Urban Wildlife, 10921 Trotting Ridge Way, Columbia, MD 21044. You may be able to use the information to help your family make your yard more hospitable to wildlife.

● *make your backyard a wildlife habitat*
Build special birdhouses. Plant flowers that bees and butterflies love. Keep fresh water out in the wintertime. And even compost leaves and food scraps so worms can eat too! The point is your backyard can be a place animals love to visit. For more ideas, write: National

Wildlife Federation, Backyard Wildlife Habitat Program, 1412 16th St. NW, Washington, DC 20036-2266.

A man is ethical only when life, as such,
is sacred to him, that of plants
and animals as that of his fellow men,
and when he devotes himself helpfully
to all life that is in need of help.
—Dr. Albert Schweitzer

Mother Earth
Needs You, Too

the word *ecology* comes from two Greek words, *oîkos*, which means "house," and *lógos*, which means "word" or "thought." So ecology refers to the study of our house, the place where we live, the world. For years people thought the world was so big that they could do anything to it and it wouldn't matter. But now we've learned that's not true. Everything we do to the Earth matters. Even when we drive to the mall, the exhaust from the car affects the air that surrounds the Earth.

Entire species of animals have been exterminated, or reduced to so small a remnant that their survival is doubtful. Forests have been despoiled by uncontrolled and excessive cutting of lumber; grasslands have been destroyed by overgrazing. . . . We have much to accomplish before we can feel assured of passing on to future generations a land as richly endowed in natural wealth as the one we live in.

—Rachel Carson

Millions of kids are concerned about the future of our planet. Kids care—and they have often helped find solutions by making the adults around them aware of environmental problems. Grown-ups listen to kids because they know kids will inherit a mess if people don't get to work now. There are lots of ways you can make our ecology, our Earth home, safer and better for you, your parents, and the children *you* may have someday.

Be a real-life Johnny Appleseed
● *"Releaf" for relief from pollution*
More than a hundred schoolchildren, their teachers, and town officials in New Orleans, Louisiana, had a tree-planting party in a city park. The trees help fight city pollution. Tree leaves capture carbon dioxide from car exhaust and convert it to oxygen for us to breathe. These trees were also important historically and were donated by the American Forestry Association's Famous and Historic Tree Program. One tree, a catalpa, was a descendant from Monticello, Thomas Jefferson's estate in Virginia. One seed came from the Valley Forge sycamores under which George Washington and his troops slept. There was also a moon sy-

camore grown from a handful of seeds carried into space by astronaut Stuart Rosa. To keep in the spirit of the Louisiana delta, some of the kids even dressed up like alligators to help! Global Releaf, a program of the American Forestry Association, will send you information on how you can plant trees (including trees of our history) and care for them in your community. Write: Global Releaf, P.O. Box 2000, Washington, DC 20013. (800) 368-5748.

You smash it . . . and I'll build around it.
—John Lennon

● **start a tree nursery**
At the Chaparral Middle School in Diamond Bar, California, sixth graders established their own nursery using money collected by recycling aluminum. The tree nursery now has more than seven hundred seedlings planted and cared for by students. Global Releaf (see address above) will tell you how you too can start a tree nursery.

● *hug a tree*

Girl Scouts in Putnam County, New York,
wanted to make sure large old trees
were both cared for and kept safe from
chain saws. They called the libraries in
their county and asked for help in locat-
ing big trees in each town. Then, the
Scouts called their member of Congress
and asked him to meet them at one of
the oldest and biggest trees in the area.
A photo was taken by a newspaper re-
porter with everyone standing in a circle
around the tree. The photo was printed
in all the local papers. The publicity
made people more aware of the big trees
in their community.

● *plant a forest in your town!*

When twelve-year-old Joseph Ziskovsky
read that the Earth needed billions of
trees, he decided to plant thousands in
his town. He called his idea Project Oxygen, and with the help of his Scout
troop, he sent letters to all the children
in elementary schools in Shoreview,
Minnesota. Then they wrote to the adult
service organizations in town and talked
to the local nursery owners. Joe got more
than 3,125 people to help him plant 3,474
trees in a twelve-square-mile area near
his hometown. Joe proved that a kid with
a lot of determination can accomplish

miracles. He was given a Point of Light award by President Bush in 1990. To find out how you can plant one or one thousand trees, write to Global Releaf (see page 86). You can also write: Tree People, 12601 Mulholland Dr., Beverly Hills, CA 90210; and National Arbor Day Foundation, Arbor Lodge 100, Nebraska City, NE 68410.

● *be a Tree Musketeer*
Tree Musketeers is a national network of kids who plant trees everywhere—from residential neighborhoods to sewage treatment plants. Instead of blaming industries for polluting the air, they form partnerships with companies to take positive action together. On Earth Day 1990, Tree Musketeers showed adults from Chevron Oil Company the proper way to plant trees and shrubs along beach dunes in El Segundo, California. Tree

Musketeers has a telephone hotline. You can call (800) 473-0263 for their newsletter; if you like, you can join up. Or write: Tree Musketeers, 406 Virginia St., El Segundo, CA 90245.

● *care for a tree or plant*
After trees or shrubs are planted in cities and towns, they need attention. Kids have volunteered in many communities to make sure plants get the water they need and are kept free from vines and weeds. You can also be a watchdog for city trees. If you see a tree that appears sickly, inform the proper person or authority. Each city or town makes its own arrangements for planting and caring for trees. Find out who is in charge by calling the administrative office of your town, which is listed in the blue pages of the phone book. Talk to this person. The tree will be glad you did.

● *save the rainforest*
In Swedish, it's *Barens Regnskog*. In Japanese it's *Nippon Kodomo No Jungle*. In English it's Save the Rainforest. Children around the world are saving thousands of acres of rainforest in the mountains of Monteverdo, Costa Rica. They have raised enough money to buy 18,000 acres

there, and the area is now called the Children's Rainforest. Some kids have even gone to visit their rainforest in Costa Rica. To find out how you can help save more of the rainforest, write: Rainforest Alliance, 270 Lafayette St., Suite 512, New York, NY 10012. (212) 941-1900. You can also adopt an acre of rainforest in the Sierra de las Minas rainforest in Guatemala. To find out how, write: Earth's Birthday Project, Packer Collegiate Institute, 170 Joralemon St., Brooklyn, NY 11201. (718) 834-0516.

Sample Press Release

School name
School address
Phone number
 For information, contact:
 Name and phone number of school contact person
News Release: Date

FOR IMMEDIATE USE

(—) Grade Collecting Pennies to Save the Rainforest in Central America

The students in the (—) grade at (school name) are conducting a penny drive to save the Sierra de las Minas rainforest in Guatemala. For every 3,500 pennies they collect, they can "adopt" an acre of rainforest and save it from being cut down for timber or burned for agriculture. Students are asking that concerned citizens collect all the pennies in jars, drawers, and banks in their homes and bring them to the school during the week of (date) to (date) from (time) in the morning to (time) in the afternoon. The school is located at (address).

On (date), Penny Day, the students will count and wrap the pennies. At (time) an armored car from the (name of bank) will pick up the pennies and take them to the bank. The president of the bank, (name), will present the students with a certified check for the pennies on (date) at (time) at the bank at (bank address).

The penny drive is part of a nationwide program sponsored by the Nature Conservancy and the Earth's Birthday Project. Schoolchildren all over the United States will be raising funds through penny collections, bake and plant sales, and raffles to buy land in the rainforest and help turn it into a nature preserve and park.

A day at the beach—working
● *see you at the beach*
Every year thousands of people go to the beach—just to clean up other people's trash! They know that a beach littered with trash is a depressing sight but that a beach lined with volunteers armed with garbage bags and eager to clean up is a positive, hope-filled sight. So they participate in citizen beach clean-ups by collecting marine debris. They also keep records of what they find and what animals are harmed by the garbage. Recently hundreds of kids in North

Carolina helped clean up 350 miles of beach. They collected more than 330,000 pounds of beach litter, most of which they were able to recycle. To find out about beach cleanups, or to receive an activity book for kids for $1, write: North Carolina Sea Grant Program, 1911 Building, Box 8605, North Carolina State University, Raleigh, NC 27695-8605. (919) 515-2454.

● *plaster posters against plastic*
Plastics in the ocean cause damage to sea life. You can help educate kids and adults in your community about this problem by hanging posters in your schools, libraries, or other public places. You can make these posters yourself, or you can order them already made from the NOAA (National Oceanic and Atmospheric Administration) Marine Debris

Information Office. One poster shows
Popeye saying, "I hope ya swabs won't
be throwin' no PLASTICS overboard!" Another poster says, "Don't teach your trash
to swim." Write NOAA's Marine Debris
Information Center at their Pacific Coast
office: 312 Sutter St., Suite 607, San Francisco, CA 94108. (415) 391-6204. Or write
to the organization at its Atlantic/Gulf
Coast office: 1725 DeSales St. NW, Washington, DC 20036. (202) 429-5609. NOAA
will also tell you where you can call to
join a beach cleanup day in your area.

● *give a show for fish*
Volunteer to give a slide show to your
class at school. Research how marine
debris hurts animals, and write a report
that you can present to others. You can
give your report to fellow students or to
members of adult groups, such as the
Rotary or PTA. You can get information
and free slide shows and videos from the
Marine Debris Information Center (see
address above).

Be bold—and mighty forces
will come to your aid.
—Basil King

Start a club to save the planet

● *start a club for Mother Earth*

At the age of eleven, a Minnesota boy
named Clinton Hill started the Kids for
Saving Earth club, which now has over
250,000 members worldwide. Kids in the
club try to find ways to cut down on energy use at home and at school. They
have gone to the United Nations and
other international organizations to talk
about their concerns. They have marched
in parades, cleaned up parks, and peti-
tioned large corporations. Clinton Hill
died of cancer when he was twelve, but
he had planted a seed of inspiration
among his friends and classmates. To
start your own Kids for Saving Earth
club, write or call: Kids for Saving Earth,
P.O. Box 47247, Plymouth, MN 55447. (612)
525-0002.

● *become an Earth Ranger*

Russell Essary, a student in Queens,
New York, was one of the founders of
KiDS S.T.O.P. (Kids Save the Planet). On
a hot summer day when his father
wouldn't turn on the car air conditioner
because of the release of CFCs, eight-
year-old Russell began to ask questions.
What were CFCs? How did they get in
air conditioners? How did they get out of

air conditioners? Russell formed a club called Earth Rangers to find out more. The Earth Rangers learned that CFCs (chlorofluorocarbons) are man-made chemicals used in refrigerators, air conditioners, and some plastic foams used to make egg cartons, cups, and fast-food cartons. CFCs drift up into our outer atmosphere and cause holes in the layer of ozone that protects the Earth. The Earth Rangers wrote their city councilman to urge him to pass laws restricting the use of CFCs. They testified at a hearing of New York City's Environmental Protection Committee regarding the release of CFCs during automobile air-conditioning repair. They spoke, presented diagrams of the ozone layer, and displayed pictures. Their work eventually resulted in a New York State law banning CFC emissions during auto repairs. Since then Earth Rangers have testified at the New York State Assembly and in the United Nations. Earth Rangers received the National Environmental Youth Award from President Bush in 1990. To start your own club, you need at least three other kids. Write KiDS S.T.O.P. at P.O. Box 471, Forest Hills, NY 11375 and send a self-addressed envelope for a reply.

Many of life's failures are people
who did not realize how close they were
to success when they gave up.
—Thomas Edison

● **start an anti-pollution club**
Melissa Poe, a ten-year-old from Nashville, Tennessee, wrote a letter to President Bush asking what he was doing
about pollution. When he didn't respond,
she asked her newspaper to publish her
letter. An advertising firm read the letter
and put it on a billboard next to a
nearby expressway. At school she
started Kids FACE—Kids for a Clean Environment. The club studies sources of
pollution, writes government officials to
encourage them to pass anti-pollution
laws, and organizes recycling efforts.
Melissa tells friends, "Kids can make a
difference. You just have to start doing
it!" Find out how to start your own chapter by writing: Kids FACE, P.O. Box
158254, Nashville, TN 37215.

Join up!
● **join the Natural Guard**
The Natural Guard sponsors pollution
patrols, energy conservation, urban trail
building, and wildlife habitat enhance-

96

ment. The organization is made up of school-age (K–12) kids who start programs for the entire community. The Natural Guard was founded by singer Richie Havens and has chapters all over the United States. If you want to plant trees, be on a pollution patrol, or be a weather watcher or a recycler with the Natural Guard, write: The Natural Guard, Inc., 2631 Durham Rd., North Guilford, CT 06457. (203) 457-1302.

● *join the Children's Earth Fund*
In 1991 the Children's Earth Fund launched "Beat the Heat: The CO_2 Challenge." CO_2 (carbon dioxide) is a primary cause of global warming and is released when fossil fuels are burned. CO_2 and other gases create the greenhouse effect. They form a barrier like the windshield of a car parked in the sun, allowing light energy to pass through but trapping the rising heat. Our Earth is getting warmer—1990 was the warmest year on record! This can cause great problems throughout the world, so one million children pledged to reduce their home's CO_2 emissions by saving energy—turning out the lights in their rooms and bicycling when possible instead of being driven in an automobile. As a result, less fuel is burned and less

97

CO_2 is released into the atmosphere. The Children's Earth Fund is preparing small cardboard solar boxes to send to developing countries so people can cook their food and sterilize drinking water with solar energy—instead of burning fossil fuels. Find out how you can join by writing: Children's Earth Fund, 40 W. 20th St., 11th floor, New York, NY 10011.

> *Tomorrow is the most important thing*
> *in life. Comes into us at midnight*
> *very clear. It's perfect when it arrives*
> *and it puts itself in our hands.*
> *It hopes we've learned something*
> *from yesterday.*
> —John Wayne

Recycling
- *be the family recycler*

Anna Ortiz of Marana, Arizona, is the family recycler. She collects and rinses out bottles and cans, then puts them out for pickup or gets someone to help her take them to the recycling center.

Eleven-year-old Dee Barton of Cold
Spring, New York, says, "For science I
have to do a recycling project at my
house to save the environment. It makes
me feel good, and it's fun!"

Use it up . . . wear it out.
Make it do . . . or do without.
—United States World War II message

- **start a "Yackety-yak—Take It Back"
  program in your school**
Ten thousand schools in the United
States are part of a national recycling
program that your school can join. The
Take It Back Foundation promotes public
awareness about environmental problems, especially the solid waste crisis.
The foundation will send you a video
made by music stars (you might have
seen it on MTV) for $12.93 if you call 1-
800-424-2843. Your teacher can order a

99

free guide with ideas for starting a
Yackety-yak program by writing: Take It
Back, 111 North Hollywood, Burbank, CA
91505. (818) 559-3391.

- **make sure your class is planning to
  celebrate the Earth's birthday**

The Earth needs your love and care—so
why not hold an annual celebration of
the Earth's birthday on April 22, Earth
Day? The Earth's Birthday Project will
help you celebrate and save rainforests
at the same time. The organization will
send you ideas about painting murals,
writing plays, and having special rainforest parties. To learn how to have a
big Earth birthday party, write: Earth's
Birthday Project, Packer Collegiate Institute, 170 Joralemon St., Brooklyn, NY
11201. (718) 834-0516.

Earth's Birthday Pledge

*Because the Earth is my home and needs
my help to survive, I will try my best
to respect it at all times by recycling,
conserving energy, saving water, and
buying and using products that are least
harmful to the environment. I also promise
to remind my friends and family to care
for the Earth in the same way.*

● *check your H_2O*
In Delaware, students and teachers are
checking the quality of their streams.
They received monitoring kits with instructions on how to check water quality
from the Du Pont company. They have
"stream watch" projects and make regular visits to wastewater treatment plants.
To find out how you can start such a
project, write: Water Quality Partnership:
Adopt-a-School Program, E.I. du Pont de
Nemours & Co., Inc., 400 Woodland Rd.,
Seaford, DE 19973.

● *be your family's "turner outer" and
"shutter offer"*
Turn out lights that are left on and make
sure faucets aren't dripping. You'll save
your family money and the Earth's energy, too.

Other ways to save the Earth
● *keep informed*
By subscribing to the kids' environmental
monthly magazine *P3/The Earth-based
Magazine for Kids*, you'll learn lots of
ways to volunteer for the planet. P3
stands for the Earth—the third planet
from the sun. A one-year subscription
costs $14. Write to: P3, P.O. Box 52,
Montgomery, VT 05470.
    Another wonderful magazine, *Ranger
Rick*, has many Earth-saving ideas, as

101

well as an Earth saver checklist. To subscribe, send $12 to: Ranger Rick, National Wildlife Federation, 1412 16th St. NW, Washington, DC 20036-2266.

● *network with other students*
You can get an action guide for environmental activism that tells you how to form environmental clubs or clubs to save animals. It also gives you names of other students who will exchange ideas with you. Called the *Student Action Guide*, it is free if you write: National Association for Humane and Environmental Education, 67 Salem Rd., East Haddam, CT 06423. (203) 434-8666.

My philosophy is that not only are you
responsible for your life,
but doing the best at this moment puts you
in the best place for the next moment.
—Oprah Winfrey

Hands Across the Water:
Helping Friends
Around
the World

television makes us aware of our planet as one big home for all of us. When there's trouble in China, we see it that day on TV. We see floods and tidal waves sweeping over Bangladesh, and we see hungry people in Ethiopia. We also see our own supermarkets filled with food while people in Eastern Europe stand in line for hours for a loaf of bread. If the world has become so small, why can't we share our plenty with people who have so little? We can, but the gift of food and clothing usually needs to be made through large international organizations. In our small world, it sometimes takes many helping hands to accomplish things.

I am ready to say to every human being,
"thou art my brother," and to offer him
the hand of concord and amity.
—Thomas Jefferson

Working with international organizations

● *skip a meal to help the hungry*
In Orlando, Florida, students skipped one meal or snack a day and donated the money saved to help feed the hungry overseas. The students sent their money to CARE, an organization dedicated to fighting world poverty and hunger. For every dollar the students raised, CARE was able to give $10 toward international relief. CARE's headquarters are at 660 First Ave., New York, NY 10016. The phone number is 1-800-521-CARE. CARE will send you information about how you can help or tell you the nearest CARE office where you can get information.

● *be a human rights activist*
Amnesty International is an organization that fights to protect such human rights as freedom of speech, freedom of assembly, freedom of religion, and voting rights. It works for the release of political prisoners and an end to torture and executions. Through Amnesty International's "Action Alert," students throughout the United States are learning that people—sometimes even kids—are imprisoned, forced to serve in the military, or even killed without reason in

some countries. They know that a "stamp can stop it." For instance, middle school students in Gallup, New Mexico, wrote to President Corazon Aquino of the Philippines to tell her about twelve-year-old Enrique Calima, who was arrested and forced to join the army. Their letter worked. Enrique Calima was released four months later. You can write to save lives too. For a free video and more information, write: Amnesty International, Urgent Action Network/CE, P.O. Box 1270, Nederland, CO 80466-1270.

Cathedral Elementary
406 Park Avenue
Gallup, NM 37301
February 11, 1991

President Corazon Aquino
Malacanang Palace
Manila
THE PHILIPPINES

Your Excellency,

We are the sixth-grade students at Sacred Heart Cathedral School. It has come to our attention that Cherry Mendoza, Cecilia Sanchez, and Enrique Calima were arrested in sitio Kanawan, barangay Binaritan, Morong, Bataan by members of the Philippine Constabulary and the Philippine Army.

We are especially concerned about Enrique Calima, age 12, who was forced to accompany on military operations under the threat of mistreatment.

Your Excellency, we would be very grateful if you would investigate this situation and all instances where young children might suffer at the hands of soldiers. Thank you.

Respectfully,

Theresa Osayande
Elizabeth Feeney
Erica Chicharello
Allen Martinez

● *make puppets to help health workers in India*

In India, health care workers use puppets to teach basic rules of nutrition and sanitation. For example, they might use the puppets to show parents how to apply medicine and bandages or how to give bottles with sterilized water to babies. Volunteers here in the United States make these puppets. You can order a kit with patterns and directions for making the puppets by sending $6 to: International Service Association for Health (INSA), P.O. Box 15086, Atlanta, GA 30333. The organization will also lend you a video showing how puppets are made and used.

• *adopt a goat*

Through INSA (International Service Association for Health) you or your Scout troop or class can adopt a goat to place with a Haitian family. INSA will give a pregnant goat to a family in Haiti in your name. This goat will provide the Haitian family with milk, cheese, and perhaps meat. The family keeps male kids, but when the goat has a female kid it is given to another family to raise for milk and cheese. Goats do well in the mountainous Haitian countryside and are perfect animals for farmers there. To obtain a video and brochure about how to adopt a goat, write to INSA at the address on previous page.

America helps the whole world
in the material field, but the time has come
for America to help
in the spiritual way also.
—Swami Satchidinanda

● *give a hunger banquet*
Your class can learn about hunger
through firsthand experience. It will help
you understand the plight of millions of
people in the world who go hungry every
day. Divide into three groups. The first
group will eat as much junk food as possible in one day, the second will eat
simple but nutritious food, and the third
group will eat only rice and drink water.
On the next day, compare how you feel,
the cost of the different foods you ate,
the amount of packaging the food came
in, and how many animals or how much
energy was used to prepare it. You can
also figure out how much money you
spend each week on junk food, and how
far that amount could go in providing
simple, nutritious food to people in a developing country. You can raise and contribute this amount of junk food money to
OXFAM (an organization that was
formed in 1942 in England as the Oxford
Committee for Famine Relief). OXFAM
produces and distributes educational
materials on issues of development and
hunger, because the organization recog-
nizes that awareness of the problems
leads to financial support for its programs. OXFAM will suggest other ways
for you to help if you write: OXFAM, 115
Broadway, Boston, MA 02116. (617) 482-1211.

- **be a brother or sister to a needy child far away**

For under $25 you and your Scout troop or Sunday school class can adopt a child in another country. You will receive a picture of the child and his/her family, and you can exchange letters. There are numerous organizations that sponsor foster children from abroad. Two organizations are: The Pearl S. Buck Foundation, Green Hills Farm, Perkasie, PA 18944. (800) 242-2825; and Save the Children Federation, 54 Wilton Rd., Westport, CT 06880. (800) 243-5075.

> *No man is an island, entire of itself;*
> *every man is a piece of the continent,*
> *a part of the main.*
>
> —John Donne

- **be a sister city**

Sue Blake and her husband, Stephen, saw a TV program about the drought in Burkina Faso, a country in West Africa. They thought that the people in their town of Decatur, Georgia, could do a lot to help the people in Africa. They contacted Sister Cities International, and soon Decatur had two sister cities,

Ouagadougou and Bousse! Most people in Decatur had never heard of these cities, but soon Decatur citizens were raising money to help build water reservoirs in Ouagadougou and exhibiting children's art from Bousse. With the support of your parents or teachers, suggest to local officials that your city or town become a sister city with a city far away. Your town can raise funds to help build schools or drill wells in the sister city— and perhaps you can even exchange visits. To learn more, write: Sister Cities International, 120 S. Payne St., Alexandria, VA 22314. (703) 836-3535.

● *buy a fence for a farm*
As you read in Chapter Three, many children carry boxes with them on Halloween to collect money for UNICEF (United Nations International Children's Fund). UNICEF can help you help poor children around the world in other ways, too. For example, if you and your friends raise $45, UNICEF can buy fencing for a poultry farm that provides meat and eggs for a village in Guatemala. For more UNICEF ideas, write: U.S. Committee for UNICEF, 333 E. 38th St., New York, NY 10016. (212) 686-5522.

● *make a friendship box*
Fill a small box with friendly gifts such as crayons, soap, combs, yo-yos, hair clips, or marbles. You can also include homemade items such as small bean-bags, bookmarks, or finger puppets. The American Red Cross will send you boxes to fill and will mail them to needy children throughout the world. You can order twenty-five empty boxes from a local chapter of the Red Cross. The Red Cross will also send the filled boxes to a country you choose. For more information, write: American Red Cross, National Headquarters, International/Youth Services, Attn: Friendship Boxes, Washington, DC 20006.

On your own
● *be a pen pal*
When you mail a letter or a package to someone in a far-off country and get a note from a new friend thousands of miles away, you feel terrific! To find a pen pal, write or call: World Pen Pals,

1690 Como Ave., St. Paul, MN 55108. (612) 647-0191. The purpose of World Pen Pals is to promote international understanding and friendship through correspondence. The organization lists more than forty thousand names of people worldwide who would like to be pen pals. One of them can be yours!

You can also get the name of a pen pal from: For Our Children's Sake, 475 Riverside Dr., Suite 828, New York, NY 10115. Send a stamped, self-addressed envelope and the organization will send you the name of your pen pal right away. Or write to: Worldwide Friendship International, 3749 Brice Run Rd., Suite A, Randallstown, MD 21133. They'll send pen pal names, too.

The thing always happens that you really believe in; and the belief in a thing makes it happen.
—Frank Lloyd Wright

● **be a scout for international friendship**
There are probably people in your community who have relatives or friends in a foreign country. If you tell people you are looking for a pen pal, or someone

who may need small gifts from time to time, you are likely to hear about someone very quickly. Today there are many children, particularly in Eastern Europe, who would love to get letters and gifts from you. Scout around.

It is better to light one candle
than curse the darkness.
—Motto of the Christopher Society

Uncle Sam
Needs
You!

if you believe in a particular solution to a problem, one of the best things you can do is to convince others to think the way you do—so they'll get busy helping to solve the problem, too. You and your friends can persuade government officials to change laws to improve the environment, health care, schools, parks, and unsafe streets. By learning how to make your voice heard, you can actually change the government.

The Quakers have a saying, "Speak truth to power." As a kid, you can do this very effectively. Elected officials like to hear from kids, and they like to quote you in their speeches. So, if you think you know the answer to a problem, let your voice be heard!

Ask not what your country can do for you, ask what you can do for your country.
—John F. Kennedy

Write a letter/make a phone call

• *use the power of the press*

When you write an official, tell about problems you are concerned with. If appropriate, tell how you've volunteered. Sometimes you may voice your opinion on how an official should vote or suggest something he/she might do. Say that you are sending a copy of your letter to the editor of your local newspaper. This lets others know your views and helps you get a quick response from elected officials.

• *write to local officials about your community*

If you think your town should organize a special project such as a cleanup drive or the establishment of a park, write your top town official. Find out this person's job title: mayor, town manager, or supervisor. This person's office is usually in the town hall. If you're not sure, look in the blue pages of your phone book under "Local government offices, city, town, and village." Your town should be listed with this person's work address and phone number. Make sure you spell the official's name correctly and write a neat, clear letter.

- *lobby your state officials*

Students in Salt Lake City, Utah, testified in the Utah legislature in support of a hazardous waste superfund bill—a bill to clean up hazardous waste. With their sixth-grade teacher, they went to the state capital to lobby for the bill's passage. They gave each legislator a flyer— a one-page document with the name and number of the bill, the name of the legislator sponsoring it, the kids' names, and the reason they thought the bill was a good idea. The kids from Utah were even able to testify on the floor of the state senate.

You don't have to go to the state capital to lobby—you can do it by phone! If you know of a bill that is up for a vote in your state legislature, you can call the office of your representative and say whether you think the bill should be passed. You will probably talk to a leg-

islative assistant, and your opinion will
be recorded. Don't forget: Your government representatives represent *you*, and
they want to know what you think. When
you call, remember these important
things:

1. Get permission from your parents if you
   want to make a long-distance call.
2. State your name and where you live.
3. Say that you support or oppose a particular bill. Give the name and number
   of the bill if you know it—but if you
   don't, simply describe the bill.
4. Explain why you support or oppose the
   bill.
5. Thank the person you are speaking with
   before you say good-bye.

● *write to the president, your senator, or
  congressperson*
Some problems are so big that only our
federal government officials in Washington can help. If, for example, you worry
that the hole in the ozone layer is growing too big, that we need to send more
help to children living in poor Third
World countries, or that our leaders
aren't working hard enough for world
peace, write and tell them! Write to the
president: President (name), The White
House, Washington, DC 20500. Write

your senator: Senator (name), U.S. Senate, Washington, DC 20510. Send a letter to your congressperson: Congressperson (name), U.S. House of Representatives, Washington, DC 20515. How can you find out the name of your senator or congressperson? Easy! Ask your public or school librarian! Or, look up the information in the *Congressional Directory* or the *Almanac of American Politics*, two books that are updated each year and can be found in most public libraries.

● *make a phone call*
Politicians, manufacturers, the media, and people in your community want to know what you think about important issues. People are often asked to call into a radio talk show or make a 900-number phone call by television news commentators. This is a great way for your voice to be heard! It costs money to make a long-distance phone call or dial a 900 number, so be sure to ask your parents for permission to make the call. You could also raise the money ahead of time for this purpose. When you call, state your name, age, and opinion. Say that you want the voice of young people to be heard. You can also call elected officials for information and to tell them what you think.

How to write a letter

When you write to government officials, you can use the format of this sample letter to get you started.

```
                              Your name
                              School or group name
                              (if necessary)
                              Street address
                              City, state, and ZIP code
                              Date

Name of person you are writing to
Title
Name of organization
Street address
City, state, ZIP code

Dear *(name):

   (Your message) ----------------------------------
   --------------------------------------------------
   --------------------------------------------------
   ------------------------------------- .
      --------------------------------------------
   --------------------------------------------------
   --------------------------------------------------
   ------------------------- .
                              Sincerely yours,
                              Your name
                              Your age and/or grade
```

*Put title here, if appropriate: President ____, Mayor ____, Honorable ____, Mr. ____, Mrs. ____, Ms. ____.

Testify and test

• *testify before government officials*
Students in New Jersey formed a group
called Kids Against Pollution (KAP). They
networked with students in other states
and organized letter campaigns to government officials. Some of the kids ap-
peared before legislators in state capi-
tals, and at a hearing held by the
Environmental Protection Agency in
Washington, DC. They are advocating
passage of an amendment to the Consti-
tution guaranteeing the right to clean
air, water, and land to everyone. These
students won a Take Pride in America
award in 1990 from President Bush. If
you want to be a member of KAP, send
$6 to KAP, P.O. Box 775, Closter, NJ
07624. KAP will send you a membership
packet with information on how to start
your own chapter and how to submit articles for the organization's newsletter.

• *test the president and send him a
report card*
Let the president know what you think
by sending him a report card. List all the
responsibilities you expect the president
of the United States to fulfill, and then
give a grade for each one. You can
grade the president on how he is doing
in areas such as world peace, the envi-

122

ronment, and civil rights. Design the report card to look like ones you receive at school.

Become a star and shine a light on someone

- *become a star*

If you and your school classmates want to learn more ways to volunteer, write to STARSERVE. This organization will send your teacher a starter kit complete with posters, activities, and suggestions for volunteer service. STARSERVE wants to hear about your volunteer activities so it can tell other kids what you are doing. For a free starter kit, ask your teacher to write: STARSERVE, P.O. Box 34567, Washington, DC 20043. (800) 888-8232.

> *I have a dream. . . .*
> —The Rev. Martin Luther King, Jr.

- *shine a light on someone*

You can nominate another kid or an adult who has helped you for a Daily Point of Light award. This presidential award is given every day of the week except Sunday to someone who has made a difference in his/her community by volunteering time and service for a favorite cause. Winners get a letter from the president and, if he visits an award winner's town, he meets with them. To nominate someone, write a letter about what that person has done and mail it to: Office of National Service, The White House, Washington, DC 20500, Attn: Daily Points of Light.

● *stick your neck out!*
The Giraffe Project, an organization that inspires people to "stick their necks out for the common good," is looking for "everyday heroes" both old and young around the world who have contributed special services to their communities. They will send your teacher teaching kits with ideas for activities kids can do, a video, and a collection of short stories about kids and adults who help others. They also want to hear about special people you know who have volunteered and made a difference. Write to: Giraffe Project, Education Dept., P.O. Box 759, Langley, WA 98260. (206) 321-0757.

*I am not bound to win, but I am bound
to be true. I am not bound to succeed,
but I am bound to live up
to what light I have.*
—Abraham Lincoln

When Money Talks Loudest: Fund-Raising Ideas

often the best way kids can help a
▓▓▓▓▓▓▓▓▓▓ cause is by contributing
money. This can also be the most fun
way to help because you can put your
skills and ingenuity to work. Think of
something you and your friends like to
do. Bake? Ride bikes? Draw pictures?
Sing? Once you've figured out what you
like to do best, think of how you can use
your skills to raise money. The following
general ideas can guide your thinking.
Many of these ideas have been applied
by kids.

There are four basic ways to raise
money: (1) sell your talents, (2) redeem
pledges, (3) do a goodwill job, and (4) organize specific events. Donate the money
you earn to your favorite cause.

**Ways to earn money by selling your
talents**
● *sell food at games*
Sell cookies and lemonade at Little
League games and other athletic events
where parents congregate to watch their

children play. Parents usually are happy to support kids' causes. They might even like to buy decorated photocopies of your favorite cookie recipes, too.

● *sell flowers and vegetables*
If you like gardening, plant a flower and/ or vegetable garden, and sell the produce to your neighbors. Make arrangements to deliver flowers or fresh, washed salad ingredients just before dinnertime to the people in your neighborhood.

● *sell your artwork*
Display your drawings and paintings in public places where people can see them. Make a sign that says you're selling your artwork to raise money for a certain cause. Be able to describe the cause to people who ask questions. You might even have pertinent information to pass out.

Genius is one percent inspiration
and ninety-nine percent perspiration.
—Thomas A. Edison

Ways to earn money by redeeming pledges

Another approach to fund-raising is to get pledges for activities you like to do. For example, members of your swim team can get pledges from supporters for the number of laps they swim. Usually, supporters pledge anywhere from a dime to a dollar a lap. After you swim your laps, you are responsible for collecting your pledges. You tell your supporters how many laps you swam and how much they owe you. You contribute your money to your team, which contributes it to a cause team members have chosen.

These kinds of fund-raising events are called "thons." *Thon* comes from the Greek, meaning "length" or "endurance"—so a "thon" is something you do for a long distance or a long time. If you walk, run, swim, or bike, you get pledges for your miles, laps, or kilometers. If you rock or dance, you get pledges for your minutes or hours. You can also get pledges for the number of

times you do something, such as shoot
baskets or jump rope. Here are some typ-
ical "thons."

- **walkathon**
- **swim-a-thon**
- **bike-a-thon**
- **trike-a-thon**
- **dance-a-thon**
- **bake-a-thon**

Using this method of fund-raising, kids
have earned money by jumping rope,
walking, shooting baskets, bouncing
balls, and dancing. You may think of
other ways. If this sounds like fun, it is!

Ways to earn money by doing goodwill jobs

Communities often lack funds to support
extra projects that make a place special.
Municipal leaders may want flowers
planted in front of town hall, letters to
Santa answered, and litter picked up in
the park, but they may not have enough
money to pay professionals to do those
jobs. So, stop for a moment and ask
yourself: What services can you, your
family, your friends, your club, and your
class offer your community at a bargain-
basement rate?

Of course, you don't have to charge
anything. You could just do the commu-

nity work on a volunteer basis. That's fine, but this section is about earning money. What money-making, goodwill jobs can you do? Some of the following projects have been discussed earlier in the book.

- Plant a garden in a public spot
- Answer letters to Santa
- Pick up litter in the parks
- Assist in after-school programs
- Read to children in day care centers
- Clean up a vacant lot

Use the money you earn to support a good cause!

- *find a local problem and offer to help solve it*
In San Rafael, California, capeweed threatened to choke out all the other plants in the Golden Gate National Recreation Area. At the same time, eighth-grade students at the Marin Waldorf School wanted to raise money for a school trip to the Costa Rican rainforest. They decided to offer their services for a fee to pull out the capeweed. First, they sent a letter to people in the community asking for donations of $.50 to $2.00 an hour for each student's work. On the let-

ter they pasted dried capeweed leaves
and also included a poem written by a
student.

When it starts, it's small;
it creeps like a hungry cat
capeweed covers all.
—Mark Hoffman, grade 7

The kids raised lots of money and
helped the park at the same time. They
were so successful that they went on to
clean up salmon streams and remove
trash from the national seashore. In the
process they made $21,000 for their trip
to the rainforest. For more information
about how to do this kind of project,
write: Project S.W.E.A.T., Center for
Changing Systems, P.O. Box 1073, Lark-
spur, CA 94977. (415) 383-7350.

**Ways to earn money by organizing
specific events**
● *have a car wash*
A good location is a school parking lot.
The school may let you use some of their
supplies (buckets, cleanser, hoses, etc.)
if you ask ahead of time and promise to
be responsible. It helps to have a school
staff member be a part of this activity.
Post signs for your car wash in high-

131

traffic areas in the community. Post
signs with arrows on them to direct people to the school parking lot. You'll need
volunteers to wash, rinse, and wipe. Another group of volunteers on the other
side of the parking lot can raise more
money by vacuuming out the inside of
cars. A good time for a car wash is on
Saturday, when many people do errands.

If everyone gives one thread,
the poor man will have a shirt.
—Russian proverb

● **have a penny drop**
Pennies are often collected by groups to
raise money for good reason—the U.S.
Treasury estimates that there are more
than ninety-two billion pennies in various corners and containers in people's
homes. Contact a local bank to advise
you what to do with your pennies. Usually, the bank will give you supplies to
count and wrap the pennies. Have a
"Penny Day" party to wrap and deliver
the pennies to the bank.

● **add up money in a math-a-thon**
At the Robey Junior High School in Pine
Bluff, Arkansas, kids earned $1,700 for a

children's cancer hospital by doing math!
With the help of their math teachers, the
students made booklets of math problems at their grade level. Then they got
friends, relatives, and neighbors to sponsor them by pledging money for each
problem they solved correctly. Most people pledged a penny or a nickel per
math problem. Then the kids went to
work! Their parents checked the booklets, marking the number of correct an-
swers, and then the kids collected their
pledges. How's your math? Fifty-five students participated, so each student
earned an average of _____?

(Answer = $30.91)

Somebody said that it couldn't be done,
But he with a chuckle replied
That "maybe it couldn't," but he would be one
Who wouldn't say so till he'd tried.
So he buckled right in with the trace of a grin
On his face. If he worried he hid it.
He started to sing as he tackled the thing
That couldn't be done, and he did it.
—Edgar A. Guest

133

- *meadow muffin mania*

To raise money for S.A.D.D. (Students
Against Drunk Driving), students at Haldane High School in Cold Spring, New
York, sponsor an unusual and attention-
getting event! A sports field is marked
off into a grid. Each square on the grid is
assigned a number. People "adopt" a
square for a price and hope, believe it or
not, that when a local resident's pony is
released to graze upon the field, the animal will stop and drop a "meadow muffin" on their square! If so, that person
wins half of the money collected and
S.A.D.D. earns the rest.

- *put on a talent show*

In Philipstown, New York, an Episcopal
church needed a new floor in the parish
house, so kids and grown-ups decided to
have a floor show! They performed skits,
sang songs, played musical instruments,
and recited poems. The biggest hit was
a boy and his dog barking together to

the tune of "Jingle Bells." All this singing, playing, howling, and barking
raised over $5,000.

● *have a tropical rainforest bake sale*
In San Francisco, students made and
sold goodies that contained ingredients
grown in the rainforests—bananas, gua-
vas, cashews, lemons, and yams. They
made beautiful posters to advertise their
sale, which was held in front of a supermarket. If you want to have a tropical
rainforest bake sale at a supermarket or
shopping mall, get permission from the
manager first. A good time for a bake
sale is on Saturday or any other time
when most people do their grocery shopping in your area.

Whether you write, phone, run, collect
pennies, or bake, working for others
makes you feel good because you know
that you are helping to make someone
else's life better. Your volunteer efforts
make a difference in the world.
Best of all, you'll discover for yourself
that kids really *do* have power when
they decide to act! Not only do grown-
ups admire kids who are trying to help;
but also, most of them are likely to listen
to what you have to say. You can use

this power to benefit people, animals, and the world we live in. So lend a helping hand—and have fun!

People Who Can Help You Help

The following is a list of national organizations with volunteer programs for kids. These organizations may have local activities in your community. By writing or calling them, you can find out about their special programs and learn if there is a chapter near you where you can volunteer.

The organizations with an asterisk (*) do not have special kids' programs but will send information packets that you can use to create awareness.

YOUNG AMERICA CARES! (YAC!)

This is a program of the United Way of America, which supports more than 150 United Way youth programs, inspires young people to take advantage of their potential as community problem-solvers, and provides them with opportunities to act. YAC! offers extensive information and how-to pamphlets for adults working with youth in all areas of volunteer services.

UNITED WAY OF AMERICA
701 N. FAIRFAX ST.
ALEXANDRIA, VA 22314
(703) 836-7100 (ext. 445)

ORGANIZATIONS FOR THE HOMELESS

DAILY BREAD
2447 PRINCE ST.
BERKELEY, CA 94705
(510) 848-3522

HABITAT FOR HUMANITY
121 HABITAT ST.
AMERICUS, GA 31709-3498
(912) 924-6935

*NATIONAL ALLIANCE TO END HOMELESSNESS
1518 K ST. NW, SUITE 206
WASHINGTON, DC 20005
(202) 638-1526

*NATIONAL COALITION FOR THE HOMELESS
1621 CONNECTICUT AVE. NW
WASHINGTON, DC 20009
(202) 265-2371

SALVATION ARMY
799 BLOOMFIELD AVE.
VERONA, NJ 07044
(201) 239-0606

COMMUNITY SERVICE

BOYS AND GIRLS CLUBS OF AMERICA
771 FIRST AVE.
NEW YORK, NY 10017
(212) 351-5900

BOY SCOUTS OF AMERICA
P.O. BOX 152079
IRVING, TX 75015-2079

CAMP FIRE, INC.
4601 MADISON AVE.
KANSAS CITY, MO 64112-1278
(816) 756-1950

4-H YOUTH DEVELOPMENT
COOPERATIVE EXTENSION SERVICE
U.S. DEPARTMENT OF AGRICULTURE
WASHINGTON, DC 20250
(301) 961-2800

138

*GENERATIONS UNITED
% THE CHILD WELFARE LEAGUE
40 FIRST ST. NW, SUITE 310
WASHINGTON, DC 20001
(202) 638-2952

GIRL SCOUTS OF THE UNITED STATES OF
AMERICA
830 THIRD AVE.
NEW YORK, NY 10022-7522
(212) 940-7500

NATIONAL ASSOCIATION OF YOUTH CLUBS
5808 16th ST. NW
WASHINGTON, DC 20011
(202) 726-2044

*NATIONAL CENTER FOR SERVICE AND LEARN-
ING IN EARLY ADOLESCENCE
CASE/CUNY
25 W. 43rd ST., ROOM 612
NEW YORK, NY 10036
(212) 642-2947

*STARSERVE
P.O. BOX 34567
WASHINGTON, DC 20043
(800) 888-8232

YMCA OF THE USA
101 N. WACKER DR.
CHICAGO, IL 60606
(312) 977-0031; (800) USA-YMCA

YOUTH VOLUNTEER CORPS OF AMERICA
1080 WASHINGTON
KANSAS CITY, MO 64105-2216
(816) 474-5761

HEALTH ORGANIZATIONS

AMERICAN CANCER SOCIETY
90 PARK AVE.
NEW YORK, NY 10016
(800) ACS-2345

AMERICAN DIABETES ASSOCIATION
1660 DUKE ST.
ALEXANDRIA, VA 22314
(800) 232-3472

CANCER INFORMATION SERVICE
(800) 4-CANCER

THE HOLIDAY PROJECT
P.O. BOX 6347
LAKE WORTH, FL 33466-6347
(407) 966-5702

*THE LIGHTHOUSE
800 SECOND AVE.
NEW YORK, NY 10017
(212) 808-0077

MARCH OF DIMES/WALKAMERICA
233 PARK AVE. SOUTH
NEW YORK, NY 10013
(212) 353-8353

MUSCULAR DYSTROPHY ASSOCIATION
3561 E. SUNRISE DR.
TUCSON, AZ 85718
(602) 529-2000

NAMES PROJECT FOUNDATION
NAMES PROJECT QUILT
2362 MARKET ST.
SAN FRANCISCO, CA 94114
(415) 863-5511

140

NATIONAL MULTIPLE SCLEROSIS SOCIETY
733 THIRD AVE.
NEW YORK, NY 10017
(800) 624-8236

ENVIRONMENTAL AND ANIMAL

PROTECTION ORGANIZATIONS

The Public Broadcasting System (PBS) has published the *Resource Compendium,* which lists the names and addresses of many environmental organizations as well as books, videos, and ideas for classroom projects. The guide costs $10.

RESOURCE COMPENDIUM
PBS ELEMENTARY/SECONDARY SERVICE
1320 BRADDOCK PL.
ALEXANDRIA, VA 22314
(703) 739-5038

AMERICAN COMMUNITY GARDENING
ASSOCIATION
325 WALNUT ST.
PHILADELPHIA, PA 19106

*AMERICAN HORSE PROTECTION ASSOCIATION
1000 29th ST. NW, SUITE T-100
WASHINGTON, DC 20007
(202) 965-0500

*AMERICAN SOCIETY FOR THE PREVENTION OF
CRUELTY TO ANIMALS (ASPCA)
BERGH MEMORIAL VETERINARY HOSPITAL
441 E. 92nd ST.
NEW YORK, NY 10128
(212) 876-7700

DEFENDERS OF WILDLIFE
1244 19th ST. NW
WASHINGTON, DC 20036
(202) 659-9510

EARTH ISLAND INSTITUTE
300 BROADWAY, SUITE 28
SAN FRANCISCO, CA 94133-3312
(415) 788-3666

EARTH'S BIRTHDAY PROJECT
PACKER COLLEGIATE INSTITUTE
170 JORALEMON ST.
BROOKLYN, NY 11201
(718) 834-0516

*ENVIRONMENTAL DEFENSE FUND
257 PARK AVE. SOUTH
NEW YORK, NY 10010
(212) 505-2100

*FRIENDS OF THE EARTH
1629 K ST. NW
WASHINGTON, DC 20006
(202) 544-2600

GLOBAL RELEAF
P.O. BOX 2000
WASHINGTON, DC 20013
(800) 368-5748

*GREENPEACE USA
1436 U ST. NW
WASHINGTON, DC 20036
(202) 466-2823

NATIONAL ARBOR DAY FOUNDATION
ARBOR LODGE 100
NEBRASKA CITY, NE 68410

NATIONAL AUDUBON SOCIETY
950 THIRD AVE.
NEW YORK, NY 10022
(212) 832-3200
(212) 546-9100

NATIONAL OCEANIC AND ATMOSPHERIC
ADMINISTRATION (NOAA)
312 SUTTER ST., SUITE 607
SAN FRANCISCO, CA 94108

NATIONAL WILDLIFE FEDERATION
1412 16th ST. NW
WASHINGTON, DC 20036-2266

NATURAL RESOURCES DEFENSE COUNCIL
40 W. 20th ST.
NEW YORK, NY 10011
(212) 727-4400

*NATURE CONSERVANCY
1815 N. LYNN ST.
ARLINGTON, VA 22209
(703) 841-5300

PROJECT WILD
P.O. BOX 18060
BOULDER, CO 80308
(303) 444-2390

RAINFOREST ALLIANCE
270 LAFAYETTE ST., SUITE 512
NEW YORK, NY 10012
(212) 941-1900

TREE MUSKETEERS
406 VIRGINIA ST.
EL SEGUNDO, CA 90245
(800) 473-0263

*WORLD WILDLIFE FUND
1250 24th ST. NW, SUITE 400
WASHINGTON, DC 20037
(202) 293-4800

INTERNATIONAL ORGANIZATIONS

AMERICAN RED CROSS
NATIONAL HEADQUARTERS
WASHINGTON, DC 20006

AMNESTY INTERNATIONAL
URGENT ACTION NETWORK/CE
P.O. BOX 1270
NEDERLAND, CO 80466-1270

CARE
660 FIRST AVE.
NEW YORK, NY 10016
(800) 521-CARE

**INTERNATIONAL SERVICE ASSOCIATION FOR
HEALTH**
P.O. BOX 15086
ATLANTA, GA 30333

OXFAM
115 BROADWAY
BOSTON, MA 02116
(617) 482-1211

**SAVE THE CHILDREN FEDERATION
NATIONAL VOLUNTEER PROGRAM**
54 WILTON RD.
WESTPORT, CT 06880
(203) 226-7271
(800) 243-5075

U.S. COMMITTEE FOR UNICEF
333 E. 38th ST.
NEW YORK, NY 10016
(212) 686-5522

index

146

About the authors

Patricia Adams is the author of *Pocohantas*, a book for young adults, and *The Good Stepmother*, a book for parents. She was a literacy volunteer in a men's prison and now teaches college writing there. During the summer before she entered eighth grade, she volunteered to assist a social worker on home visits in rural North Carolina.

Jean Marzollo has written more than fifty books for young readers, including *Pizza Pie Slugger, Red Ribbon Rosie, Cannonball Chris,* and *Soccer Sam.* She has also written many articles and books for parents and teachers. She served as an elected trustee for ten years on her local school board. When she was in high school, she volunteered on Sundays to teach swimming to physically challenged children.

THE HELPING HANDS ESSAY CONTEST

Have you lent a helping hand?

If you answered yes, then you should enter the Helping Hands Essay Contest—you may win $1,000 for your favorite cause!

If you've given up your time to do volunteer work you're proud of, we want to hear about it.

It's easy. Just write a short essay (no more than 250 words) and tell us about how you've volunteered and why you're proud of what you've done. The author of the best essay will be our Grand Prize Winner, and we'll donate $1,000 to the cause of his or her choice!

AND the Grand Prize Winner's name and a quotation from the winning essay will appear in the next edition of *The Helping Hands Handbook**. We'll also make three $100 donations for the three runners-up!

See the official rules below.

OFFICIAL RULES—RANDOM HOUSE HELPING HANDS ESSAY CONTEST

1. No purchase is necessary. Enter by hand-printing or typing your name, address, date of birth, and telephone number on a plain 3″ x 5″ card. Send this

*Subject to Random House's publishing a further edition of the book.

card along with your essay telling us about your volunteer work, why you're proud of it, and the name of the organization to which you would want us to make a donation should you win. Send to:

Random House Juvenile
201 East 50th Street
New York, NY 10022
Attn: The Helping Hands Essay Contest

2. PRIZES

Grand Prize: A check for $1,000 will be donated to the cause/charitable organization chosen by the Essay Contest winner.

Three Runner-up Prizes: Three checks for $100 each will be donated to the causes/charitable organizations chosen by the three runners-up.

3.
Enter as often as you wish, but each essay must be original, and each entry must be mailed in a separate envelope bearing sufficient postage. All completed entries must be postmarked and received by Random House no later than March 31, 1993, in order to be eligible for the Essay Contest. The receipt of manuscripts will not be acknowledged unless a self-addressed stamped postcard is included with the submission. Entrants must be no older than 16 years old at the time of entry. Each essay must be no more than 250 words and must be typed double-spaced or neatly printed on one side of an 8½" x 11" page which has the entrant's name, address, date of birth, and telephone number at the top. At the end of the essay, write, "If I'm a winner, please make a donation to _____" and fill in the name of the cause or charitable organization where you'd like to see the money go. The Grand Prize Winner's name and a quotation, as selected by Random House, from the winning essay will appear in *The Helping Hands Handbook*, in the

event of a further edition. The essays submitted will be judged by the authors of *The Helping Hands Handbook* on the basis of originality, thoughtfulness, and writing ability, and all decisions are final and binding. Essays become the property of Random House and none will be returned. Essay Contest winners will be notified by mail on or about May 15, 1993. Winners have 30 days from the date of Random House's notice in which to respond, or another Helping Hands Essay Contest winner will be chosen. Random House is not responsible for incomplete or lost or misdirected entries.

4. The Grand Prize and the Runner-up Prizes are nontransferable and no substitutions will be allowed. If requested, winners and their parent or legal guardian agree to execute an Affidavit of Eligibility and Promotional Release supplied by Random House. Entering the Helping Hands Essay Contest constitutes permission to use the winner's name, address, likeness, and contest submission for publicity and promotional purposes, with no additional compensation.

5. Essay Contest open to residents of the U.S. and Canada, except for the province of Quebec. Employees and their families of RANDOM HOUSE, INC., and its affiliates, subsidiaries, advertising agencies, and retailers may not enter. This offer is void wherever prohibited, and subject to all federal, state, and local laws.

6. For a list of winners, send a stamped, self-addressed envelope to:

Random House Juvenile
201 East 50th Street
New York, NY 10022
Attn: The Helping Hands Essay Contest Winners